Dale

Earnhardt

Earnhardt

1951–2001

Frank Moriarty

MetroBooks

MetroBooks

An Imprint of Friedman/Fairfax Publishers

Library of Congress Cataloging-in-Publication Data available upon request

ISBN 1-56799-965-4

Editor: Nathaniel Marunas
Art Director: Kevin Ullrich
Designer: John Marius
Photography Editor: Valerie Kennedy

Printed in the United States of America

10 9 8 7 6 5 4 3 2

For bulk purchases and special sales,
  please contact:
Friedman/Fairfax Publishers
Attention: Sales Department
15 West 26th Street
New York, NY 10010
212/685-6610 FAX 212/685-3916

Visit our website:
http://www.metrobooks.com

Dedication

This book is dedicated to the talented people who cover the Winston Cup Series for ESPN, the cable sports network whose own ascension paralleled that of Dale Earnhardt and NASCAR itself. Through nearly two decades of Winston Cup coverage, ESPN defined state-of-the-art coverage of a sport that presents myriad broadcasting challenges. The networks that recently won the high-stakes financial battle for the rights to broadcast the Winston Cup Series beyond the year 2000 will find their jobs have been made much easier thanks to ESPN's trailblazing efforts. From the network's superb on-air broadcast team, anchored by Bob Jenkins and former drivers Ned Jarrett and Benny Parsons, to its brilliant technical innovations (on-car and in-car cameras, for instance), ESPN set standards that may never be matched. Every fan of the sport owes ESPN a debt of gratitude.

Acknowledgment

Special thanks to the International Motor Sports Hall of Fame's very own Betty L. Carlan, who kindly provided early shots of Ralph and Dale Earnhardt for publication in this book. Without her assistance, this tribute to Dale's amazing career would hardly be complete.

Photo Credits

Allsport: ©Jon Ferrey: 93; ©Jim Gund: 59;
  ©Craig Jones: 6; ©David Taylor: 60-61, 85

AP Photo/Wide World Photos: ©Phil Coale: 86

©Tom Bernhardt: 48-49

©Steve Haggerty: 77

International Motor Sports Hall of Fame: 7, 11, 12, 14,
  17, 30, 31

©Nigel Kinrade: 2, 63, 64, 67, 68, 70, 71, 73,
  74-75, 81, 87, 88-89, 92

©Dorsey Patrick: 27, 32, 33, 34, 35, 38-39, 66, 69

©Joe Robbins: 5

©Mike Slade: 8-9, 21, 23, 24-25, 28, 36-37, 41, 42, 43,
  44, 46-47, 51, 52, 55, 57

©Sports Chrome: 90

Sports Chrome: ©Greg Crisp: 82-83, 91;
  ©Ron McQueeney: 78-79; ©Evan Pinkus: 72

UPI/Corbis-Bettmann: 18-19

Contents

INTRODUCTION

Itt's true, this book is full of facts and figures about the career of Dale Earnhardt.

It is the story of the son of a racer, and how that young man matured while racing in NASCAR's Winston Cup Series. How he won race after race, and how he tied the record of the sport's king, Richard Petty, with seven series championships. And how he finally won NASCAR's greatest prize, the Daytona 500.

But more than just facts and figures, this book is a celebration of one of the greatest drivers to ever sit behind the wheel of a stock car. It's one thing to see in the record book that Dale Earnhardt won the 1991 Busch Clash at Daytona International Speedway on February 1, 1991. It's something else entirely to see *how* he did it—blasting from sixth to first in one lap in the race's first segment, then starting from last in an inverted field based on the results of the first segment and passing thirteen cars in two laps on his way to winning the second segment.

It's common now to see a strong car go to the front of a Winston Cup race and dominate the event. Common, and not too exciting. But when Dale Earnhardt was behind the wheel of a poor-handling stock car, that car had just become a contender.

That talent, that incredible skill and fearless approach, says more about Dale than any mere collection of facts and figures, no matter how impressive. Like many fans, I'd hoped to see Dale win an eighth championship. It won't happen now, but it is likely that he will forever remain tied with the King, Richard Petty, as one of the two greatest NASCAR Winston Cup champions of all time.

When any great career is cut short, it leaves questions of what might have been. But for more than two decades, Earnhardt's performances on NASCAR speedways gave us stories and memories that may never be equalled. As race fans, we should consider ourselves fortunate to have witnessed the legend of Dale Earnhardt's career written before our very eyes.

Opposite: The first four winners (left to right) of NASCAR's newest "great race," the Brickyard 400, held at historic Indianapolis Motor Speedway: Jeff Gordon, Dale Jarrett, Ricky Rudd, and Dale Earnhardt.

Right: He's not quite wearing a fireproof driver suit, but a young Dale Earnhardt already seemed to be looking forward to his future (and sometimes incendiary) battles in the Winston Cup Series.

THE SON OF A RACER

What is the key component of becoming a legend? Sure, the results are important, and they provide the facts that become the foundation of the story. But the real heart of any good legend, the part everyone always remembers, is how the hero accomplishes his quest.

In stock car racing, there have been many legends. It's a sport that has celebrated its first fifty years with a cast of colorful characters and wild stories. There's Tim Flock, racing around NASCAR's early tracks with a monkey scampering about inside the car. There's Cale Yarborough and the Allison brothers, fighting in the infield at Daytona before a live television audience over a chance for victory that fell into the lap of Richard Petty. There's Alan Kulwicki, guiding an underfunded team to the Winston Cup Series championship, beating out the race teams everyone expected to win.

But one of the greatest legends of stock car racing concerns the Intimidator, Dale Earnhardt, who had gained mythical status long before his fatal crash on the final lap of the 2001 Daytona 500. Dale's story is one of a man who grew up virtually a son of the sport itself, using his talent to rise up from humble beginnings to become possibly the greatest driver the sport has ever seen—or ever will see.

"I drive a race car a hundred percent every race," Dale Earnhardt once said, "and that is what I intend to do until I retire."

In the world of the modern NASCAR Winston Cup Series, where million-dollar race bonuses are posted, where condominiums are built high above grandstands, where drivers arrive at racetracks with briefcases in tow, Dale Earnhardt's notion of driving a race car one hundred percent at all times almost seemed like an attitude from the past. And in a way, it was.

Dale Earnhardt was born on April 29, 1951. His family's home was in Kannapolis, North Carolina, a town in Cabarrus County, northeast of Charlotte. When Dale was born, one of the main sources of income in Kannapolis came from the textile industry. But in the Earnhardt household, the main focus was on racing. Dale was the family's oldest son, later joined by brothers Danny and Randy, and sisters Kathy and Kay.

Dale's mother, Martha, once expressed amazement at the success Dale had: "It is really awesome for me sometimes when I look at the TV and there's my son in a commercial. Everywhere you look, there he is. I go into a grocery store and there he is on a cereal box. It's hard to comprehend sometimes how far he really has come."

But Dale's long journey to stock car racing superstardom found direction early on, and the inspiration was right at home: Dale's father, Ralph Earnhardt.

"My earliest memory is of watching daddy in a race," Dale said in 1976. "Following in his footsteps is all I've ever wanted to do."

Ralph Earnhardt was one of the great drivers on whose shoulders NASCAR stock car racing was built. In the 1950s and 1960s, he developed a fearsome reputation among Grand National drivers in the division that would one day evolve into the Winston Cup Series. Ralph was known as a tough competitor—"one of the best short-track drivers ever," in the opinion of Bobby Isaac, NASCAR's 1970 champion.

It was on the short tracks that Ralph Earnhardt's aggressive style and determination brought him the greatest success. Though he enjoyed competing against the drivers of the Grand National Series, Ralph

did not care much for the demands of traveling. Instead, he preferred to race close to home, and the North Carolina region provided him plenty of opportunities, on famed tracks like Hickory Speedway, Concord Speedway, and Richmond Fairgrounds Speedway.

Before deciding to concentrate on racing locally, Ralph won the 1956 NASCAR Sportsman championship, winning track titles at speedways up and down the East Coast. No one is sure exactly how many races Ralph won during his career, but everyone agrees that the win total is staggering.

Dale's interest in cars began when he was a child, but unlike most boys and girls who find autos fascinating, young Earnhardt had a garage in the backyard that contained an actual race car.

"I would wake up in the morning about 5:30 wanting to know how [my father] finished the night before," Dale recalled. "I would go out to the garage where daddy kept his race car. He was running dirt tracks back then, so all I had to do was look at the front end to see how he did the night before. You knew if the front end of the car was covered with dirt he was following somebody and that meant he finished second or third. Now, if the

Pages 8–9: Wrecked cars often mark the progress of a young driver breaking into NASCAR's top ranks, and Dale Earnhardt left his share of torn sheet metal behind as he matured in competition.

Above: Every little boy's dream—twenty-four-hour access to a working race car. Young Dale stands at left in front of the number 8 stock car, which belonged to Dale's dad, Ralph.

car was pretty clean you knew he had a good night and probably won the race."

Whenever he could, Dale traveled with his father to see firsthand how the car performed. Sometimes he was chased out of the pits for being too young, but he was already garnering knowledge that would serve him well throughout his life.

When not accompanying his father on racetrack adventures, Dale did what every aspiring race car driver does: he built model race cars. He also built bicycles and raced against his friends on a makeshift track. Leg power gave way to motor power when Dale became old enough to ride a go-kart, which Ralph built for his son. Dale's competitive spirit came out in other sports he played, but it was racing—who could go fastest, who could finish quickest—that most enticed him.

Dale really started his driving career doing work on farms, motoring along on tractors and behind the wheels of trucks. But naturally enough, Dale

wanted to ride something a bit more nimble. He knew he wanted to follow in his father's tracks.

"My dad was the focus of my life," Dale said. "I didn't like school. I wanted to be home working on Dad's race car. I wanted to be home working on cleaning up the shop. I would just as soon be washing wrenches. I followed him around and did everything he did."

Dale's disenchantment with school wore on him, and in 1966 he quit. Earnhardt wanted to focus on racing, but his parents were furious with the teen. Dale later admitted that leaving school showed poor judgement, but he did go to work right away at a local auto service station. He began to apply the mechanical knowledge he had acquired while he was at his father's side.

Though still displeased with his son's decision to leave school, Ralph respected Dale's determination to make it on his own, and the hard work his son put in at the service station, and later at a mill job. And he must have been proud to see Dale begin to win in short-track competition driving an old Ford Falcon race car.

"I figure I have a lot to learn," a twenty-one-year-old Dale said in 1972. "I guess it took Daddy ten years to know what he was doing. I hope I progress as rapidly as he did."

Left: At an age when he was actively helping his father—and learning what racing is all about in the process—Dale stands proudly next to Ralph (far right) during a break in the tough competition of North Carolina short-track racing.

ON HIS OWN

In the early 1970s, things were looking good for Dale Earnhardt. His father was making decent money in winnings at the short tracks of North Carolina, and Dale himself was applying the precious racing knowledge his father had passed to him, including the maxim, "There's only one lap you want to lead, and that's the last lap." People were becoming aware that Ralph wasn't the only Earnhardt with racing talent.

"There are no deep, dark secrets," Dale maintained. "That's part of the philosophy my daddy taught me: you prepare that race car the best you can, and you work hard and you run hard and you keep your composure about you, and it'll all work out. You establish your territory. And you always stay cool on the racetrack."

Earnhardt was cool on the racetrack, although some of his competitors may have been less cool after falling victim to one of Dale's aggressive charges.

Then, on September 27, 1973, tragedy struck. Dale entered the garage where his father's race cars were prepared, as he had done countless times since he was a young boy. This time, though, Dale found his father slumped over the car. Ralph Earnhardt had died of a heart attack at the age of forty-five.

The press in the Charlotte area recognized the loss the sport had suffered, recounting the highlights of hard-fought battles between Ralph and his competitors. And those competitors were quick to admit the respect they had for Dale's father, too. "If they kept records of it," the great Bobby Isaac speculated at the time, "Ralph Earnhardt has probably won more races than any other driver in the country."

And Grand National champion Ned Jarrett has described Ralph as "the most intense, hard-driven man I have ever known."

Dale, then twenty-two years old, was deeply hurt by the loss of his father, who had taught the young driver so much about how to be racer.

"I was so mad at him for leaving this world," Dale explained. "I didn't get over it for a year. I'm still not over it. There isn't a day that goes by that I don't think of my father."

Dale cherished his memories of the few times he had raced against Ralph, and he found the strength to push on in spite of his loss. He began work at Punch's Wheel Alignment in Concord, North Carolina, and set his sights on making his dreams of a racing career a reality.

Like most young drivers, Dale Earnhardt struggled to carve out a future in stock car racing. Going fast takes money, and like others before him, Dale borrowed money knowing full well that a strong showing in a weekend's race would be the only way he could pay the money back.

Operating out of the family shop, Earnhardt went from track to track, always learning, always honing his raw ability. The speedways he competed at were dirt tracks, where tough, unforgiving competition was the rule.

In 1974, young Earnhardt moved on to the Sportsman division and competed on paved racetracks. His car was purchased from Harry Gant, who like Dale would one day rise to Winston Cup stardom. But stardom was far from certain, and racing on pavement presented Dale with a whole new set of challenges. And along with the challenges came definite thrills, including Dale's first race on the imposing high banks of Charlotte Motor Speedway, where he finished in a respectable thirteenth place.

In May 1975, Dale Earnhardt tested the waters of the division his father had turned his back on. NASCAR's elite Grand National Series was now known as the Winston Cup Series, and Dale made his first start in the sport's longest race, the World 600 at Charlotte Motor Speedway. Driving a Dodge for Ed Negre, Earnhardt managed 355 laps, completing 533 miles (857.6km) of competition, before the checkered flag fell for winner Richard Petty.

It was a respectable debut. Earnhardt had started the race in thirty-third position, climbing through the field to end up in twenty-second place. For his efforts, Dale won two thousand dollars.

While Dale kept his foot in the bread-and-butter racing of the Sportsman division, he managed to log two Winston Cup starts in 1976, one for Walter Ballard and the other for Johnny Ray; he dropped out of both events. The two runs netted Earnhardt just over three thousand dollars.

Above: Dale on the verge of Winston Cup stardom. Having signed with car owner Rod Osterlund, Earnhardt was about to get the equipment he needed to begin a serious assault on the Winston Cup Series.

Dale Earnhardt wasn't exactly setting the Winston Cup Series on fire, but competing in NASCAR's top division requires an education all its own. And even though the winnings were far from staggering, he was cashing his first Winston Cup checks—with many, many more to come.

A NEW BEGINNING

In 1977, Dale Earnhardt met Teresa Houston, herself part of a well-known racing family in North Carolina. Though he was finding greater and greater success on the racetrack, Earnhardt, now twenty-six years old, had not had equal success in his personal relationships. Married at seventeen and later divorced, Dale had yet to find someone to share his life in a romance that could withstand the pressures of establishing a racing career.

Racing leads to an unusual lifestyle: late hours working on the car, endless travel towing the car, the dangers of the race itself. As Dale grew closer to Teresa, he was impressed by her support and understanding. In 1982, the couple were married.

But as the 1980s neared, Dale was still trying to break into NASCAR's top ranks. In 1978, Earnhardt made some encouraging headway. Part of the credit for this initial success goes to the dubious Winston Cup non-career of Willy T. Ribbs.

Ribbs was America's best-known African American driver, whose greatest success was as a road course driver. With the aid of Charlotte Motor Speedway's Humpy Wheeler, arrangements were made for Ribbs to drive a Ford for car owner Will Cronkite. The goal was for Ribbs to compete against the Winston Cup stars in Charlotte's World 600. Wheeler even arranged for a private practice session for Ribbs in May, two weeks before the six-hundred-mile (965.4km) event. Ribbs never showed up at the track for the sessions.

"A car was available to Ribbs for two days," Cronkite said. "I felt it imperative that Ribbs log some times on the track in a big car. His not reporting for practice is contrary to my approach to racing."

Cronkite's choice to fill Ribbs' vacant seat? Dale Earnhardt.

"Dale is an extremely competitive driver," explained Cronkite. "He has the capability of putting a car up front and making it go as fast as it can."

Earnhardt was credited with a seventeenth-place finish in NASCAR's longest race, although he was relieved behind the wheel by Harry Gant. Doubtless the six-hundred-mile (965.4km) length was a tremendous change for Dale, who had come to face this daunting event fresh from the short distances of the Sportsman series.

A few weeks later, on the Fourth of July, Dale was ready to try again for Cronkite, this time at the Firecracker 400. It was his first race at a track that would bring Dale some of his greatest triumphs and biggest heartbreaks: Daytona International Speedway. After qualifying in the twenty-eighth starting position, Earnhardt raced up through the pack to claim his first top-ten finish. The race was won by David Pearson. Dale's seventh-place run was worth just under four thousand dollars.

Car owner Rod Osterlund had noticed Dale's performance in his four runs for Cronkite in the 1978 season. Late in the season, Osterlund decided to field a second car with Earnhardt at the wheel, teamed with primary driver Dave Marcis. In a controversial five-hundred-mile (804.5km) race at

Atlanta International Raceway won by Donnie Allison, Marcis and Earnhardt came home in third and fourth, respectively. Dale's first top-five did not particularly please Marcis, who did not care for Osterlund's plans for a two-car team. Earnhardt was just happy to have performed so well.

"I'd sure like to keep this ride," he said. "I think in time I could win with this car."

Driver Jimmy Insolo was seated in the second Osterlund Chevrolet at the next race, held two weeks later at California's Ontario Motor Speedway. But Earnhardt later relieved Insolo and guided the car to a seventh-place finish. By doing so, Dale kept his race starts for the season at five, retaining his eligibility to compete for the 1979 Winston Cup Series Rookie of the Year title. The Ontario race wrapped up the season, leaving Earnhardt anxiously looking forward to the year to come.

With Dave Marcis' departure, Dale Earnhardt was now Osterlund's main driver. After beginning the 1979 season on the road course at Riverside, California, with a middle-of-the-pack performance, the team moved on to the Daytona 500.

It was Dale Earnhardt's first attempt at winning the "Great American Race," and he managed to start in the tenth position. The team had switched to Buicks from Chevrolets, but Earnhardt adapted quickly and scored another top-ten, finishing in eighth place, just behind Chuck Bown. It was just the first performance in a season during which Dale surprised many of the sport's observers with the speed of his ascension to the level of Winston Cup contender.

By the time the Winston Cup Series pulled into Tennessee's Bristol International Raceway for the Southeastern 500 on April 1, Dale had built a string of strong runs. The team was running Chevrolets on NASCAR's shorter tracks, and the week before at North Wilkesboro Speedway in North Carolina, Earnhardt had rumbled to a fourth-place finish—matching his career best—after leading during the event.

At Bristol, Dale ripped off a qualifying lap good enough for ninth in the field—slower than pole winner Buddy Baker's lap of 111.668 mph (179.7kph), but fast enough to prove to the other drivers that he might well be a factor on the tight corners of the fast half-mile speedway.

When the green flag waved, Buddy Baker roared into the lead, holding off his competition for the first one hundred laps. But Baker's day came to an end when he was involved in a crash with Cale Yarborough. This day was to be Dale Earnhardt's. In just his sixteenth Winston Cup Series start, the twenty-eight-year-old driver was first to the checkered flag, leading more than 160 laps and beating runner-up Bobby Allison by three seconds.

"I'll probably believe it in the morning," the happily dazed Earnhardt said. "This is a bigger thrill than my first-ever racing victory. This win was in the big leagues.... It was against top-caliber drivers. It wasn't some dirt track back home."

The dirt tracks back home were quickly relegated to memory, as Earnhardt built on the victory with more consistent finishes. Top-fives and top-tens came with regularity for the young driver as the season raced into summer. Then an incident that threatened Dale's career befell the Osterlund team.

On July 30, Dale was leading the five-hundred-mile (804.5km) race at Pennsylvania's huge, triangular Pocono International Raceway. The cars were nearly one hundred laps into the event when one of Dale's tires failed in the track's second turn. This turn, which passes over the infield tunnel and is nicknamed The Tunnel Turn, is one of the most feared and respected in stock car racing. Earnhardt's tire failure could not have come at a worse place.

When the car finally stopped, Dale had suffered two broken collar bones, a concussion, and bad bruising. But the worst injury may have come in the form of his doctors' estimates of a six-to-eight-week recovery period. Earnhardt had been fifth in the championship points when the team arrived at Pocono for the ill-fated race.

"The doctor in charge told me that judging from the way the collar bones were broken, it was an act of God my neck wasn't broken, too," Earnhardt said weeks later. During his recovery, he anxiously watched as David Pearson filled in for him, winning the Southern 500 at Darlington along the way.

Dale finally got back behind the wheel for the Richmond, Virginia, race on September 9. He did so in style, winning the pole for the event with a 92.605-mph (149kph) lap around the half-mile track. That set the pace for the remainder of the season, as the Osterlund team wrapped up seven more top-ten finishes after Dale returned to the driver's seat.

When the final results were tallied in November, after the season finale at the Ontario track, Dale ended up seventh in championship points. One win, eleven top-fives, and seventeen top-tens was an impressive record by any standard in Winston Cup racing. For a rookie, it was amazing.

No one was surprised when he was named 1979 NASCAR Winston Cup Series Rookie of the Year. But for Dale Earnhardt, it was just the beginning.

Below: With his car carrying the number borne by his father's stock cars, Dale poses at Daytona International Speedway, the superspeedway that would be the site of Earnhardt's greatest frustrations and triumphs.

QUICK CLIMB TO THE TOP

He knew if he just got the chance, he could get the job done. And in 1979, Dale Earnhardt proved that was true beyond all doubt. When he did get his chance, Dale was a contender in almost every race and finished high in the Winston Cup championship points standings, despite being unable to race for several weeks after a bad midseason crash.

The question was not if Earnhardt could make it in Winston Cup racing, but how far he would go.

Earnhardt's winning the Rookie of the Year title convinced car owner Rod Osterlund that he was aligned with the real thing, and Osterlund wanted to keep the magic alive. Shortly after the last race of the 1979 season, Osterlund and Earnhardt came to terms on a contract.

"Rod Osterlund and I have agreed on a five-year deal with three option years, and I couldn't be more tickled," Earnhardt told *The Charlotte Observer*'s Tom Higgins. "Talk about job security, I've got it. It frees me to concentrate on winning races and going for the driving championship, and believe me, that's a tremendous plus.

"We spent last year learning each other and we're ready to go now. I expect us to make vast improvement over '79 because now we know how to work with each other."

Dale wasted no time notifying the competition that he was ready for the big time. At the season-opening race on the road course at California's Riverside International Raceway, Earnhardt demonstrated he knew how to turn right as well as left. He chased down leader Darrell Waltrip, falling just short in his quest to overtake his fellow driver.

The Winston Cup cars then crossed the country to prepare for the Daytona 500. The week before the 500, the Busch Clash is held, an all-star event for the fastest qualifiers of the previous season. The 1979 edition of the event saw Dale Earnhardt in a small but elite starting field made up of Richard Petty, Neil Bonnett, Cale Yarborough, Bobby and Donnie Allison, Harry Gant, Joe Millikan, David Pearson, Benny Parsons, Buddy Baker, and Darrell Waltrip.

In yet another race, Earnhardt found himself chasing Waltrip. But this time Dale was not to be denied. Waltrip went low down the huge backstretch at Daytona, planning on blocking Earnhardt's anticipated low pass. "Darrell wanted to shut me off, so he went to the inside," Earnhardt explained after the race. "When he did that, I went to the outside and got into the corner in turn three ahead of him."

Dale never looked back and stormed to an impressive victory televised live nationally by CBS. Earnhardt won the event with an average speed of 191.693 mph (308.4km).

"This does so much for my confidence and for the team," he said from victory lane. "We really have our act together. Now I feel certain that I can win the Daytona 500 next Sunday."

Pages 18–19: A sight that would become all too familiar to his fellow competitors–Dale Earnhardt leading a pack of cars to the finish line.

Above: When Earnhardt entered Winston Cup competition, there were no pit road speed limits. But the pit stops themselves took longer than they do today, and here Dale waits for service to be completed in 1980 competition.

He came close. Earnhardt led the race on seven separate occasions, and doubtless made race winner Buddy Baker nervous, but in the end the Osterlund Oldsmobile fell to fourth place. Still, it was a very respectable performance, and it set the team at the top of the points standings for the season-long run at the championship.

It's often said that consistency wins championships, and the Osterlund team was showing that trait early in the season. After Daytona, Earnhardt took fifth at Richmond and third at North Carolina Motor Speedway.

At the Atlanta 500, Earnhardt's stock car was balky during practice and qualifying before the race,

and the best Dale could manage was a thirty-first starting position. But the race itself was another matter entirely.

Earnhardt worked his way through the pack, finally taking the lead late in the race. Bobby Allison got back by Dale, but then Earnhardt took the lead for good with twenty-eight laps left in the event. He cruised on for his second career win, blasting across the finish line more than nine seconds ahead of the driver who came in second. That driver was making his very first Winston Cup start and would go on to become one of Dale Earnhardt's fiercest rivals: it was Rusty Wallace.

Having won his first race at Bristol the year before, Earnhardt returned to Tennessee as the defending track champion. Confidence is the foundation of strong performances, and the Osterlund team was on a roll. At Bristol, Earnhardt repeated as victor, beating Darrell Waltrip by more than eight seconds.

"I love it!" Earnhardt exclaimed after claiming his third career victory. "When I joined Osterlund, I really thought it would take a year to win my first race. But then we won this race last year and we'll win our share this year. I don't see any reason why I can't win the Grand National championship this year."

The optimism continued at the next race, even though Earnhardt's stock car suffered an engine failure 104 laps into the event at South Carolina's Darlington Raceway. Bobby Allison, second to Earnhardt in the points chase, suffered engine failure as well, and because his Ford went out of the race eighteen laps sooner than Dale's car, Earnhardt actually increased his points lead.

Dale maintained his torrid pace, scoring top-tens in every subsequent race leading to the World 600, save one. At Charlotte Motor Speedway, for the longest race of the year, Earnhardt's car was very strong, going to the front and battling with the cars of Richard Petty, Benny Parsons, and Cale Yarborough. But on lap 276, Dale's stock car blew a tire, sending him into a spin that also collected David Pearson, Bobby Allison, and Yarborough. Hard work by Dale's pit crew got him back into the race and running fast enough to salvage a twentieth-place finish.

With so much going so well, it came as a shock to the team when crew chief Jake Elder quit after the World 600. Expressing displeasure with team manager Roland Wlodyka and Osterlund, and citing a change of attitude in Earnhardt, whom Elder described as "cocky," Jake left the team just short of the halfway mark of the season.

Replacing a crew chief is something best done in the off-season, as team chemistry can be thrown off by sudden changes. But the Earnhardt team regrouped with two consecutive top-ten finishes. Doug Richert settled in as Elder's replacement.

A strong third-place run at the Firecracker 400 in Daytona set the stage for the season's second half, which quickly got better when the team arrived at Nashville International Raceway. Despite facing a stiff challenge from Cale Yarborough—including some insistent taps from the front bumper of Cale's Chevrolet—Dale Earnhardt won his third race of the season.

In late September, it was again Earnhardt versus Yarborough, as the Winston Cup Series battled at Martinsville Speedway, in southern Virginia. This time Cale had the lead, and Dale was closing in fast. But the expected battle to the checkered flag never materialized, as one of Yarborough's tires failed. Earnhardt virtually inherited his fourth win of the year.

Asked about his driving style and the points chase at Martinsville, Dale had a simple answer: "I got here by running hard and I'll continue to do that."

The next week, at Charlotte Motor Speedway, again it was Cale versus Dale. Earnhardt's crew made the difference, getting him in and out of the pits with enough of a lead to hold off Yarborough's charge.

"No one can know how much I've dreamed and thought of this moment," Dale said after winning at the superspeedway closest to his home. "It's an even better feeling than I thought it would be."

But with three races left in the season, Cale Yarborough was making a determined charge at the championship. Earnhardt still had the points lead, but Cale was experienced, determined, and on a hot streak.

At North Carolina Motor Speedway on October 19, Yarborough chalked up another win and Earnhardt was involved in two accidents; Dale settled for eighteenth place. Cale had cut Dale's points lead to a slim forty-four.

The pressure mounted at Atlanta International Raceway on November 2, when Yarborough won again. Earnhardt finished third, one lap down. Cale was furious after the race, intimating that Earnhardt had tried to intentionally hold him up late in the race when Dale was a full lap behind.

"It was the worst piece of driving I've ever seen," an indignant Yarborough stated. "He had no business running like that when he's a lap behind. I think he would have rather wrecked the both of us than have me win this race. I think the pressure for the championship is getting to him."

And there was definitely pressure. Cale's win at Atlanta moved him to within twenty-nine points of Earnhardt. The stage was set for the season's finale, at Ontario Motor Speedway. The championship would be decided in California on November 15.

Above: Earnhardt in Busch Grand National competition at Daytona. Though he often won the 300-mile (480km) February race in NASCAR's junior division, victory in the Daytona 500 driving a Winston Cup car proved to be considerably more elusive.

In The Los Angeles Times 500, Dale Earnhardt had to overcome incidents that might have finished off a lesser driver. He lost a lap on a mistimed pit stop but clawed his way back into the lead lap. Then, late in the race, disaster in the pits struck again: not all of the lug nuts were secured on Dale's car, and NASCAR black-flagged Earnhardt, forcing him back into the pits to correct the situation. Battling on, Dale stayed within striking distance of his rival Yarborough.

Benny Parsons won the race, Cale Yarborough took third, but Dale Earnhardt won fifth place—and the 1980 Winston Cup championship.

"My heart really dropped when I got black-flagged," Earnhardt admitted. "But I can't say anything bad about the crew, as hard as they've worked this year."

Looking back on his amazing season, and the championship that he won by just nineteen points, Dale knew that he had accomplished a tremendous feat for a driver in just his second year in the Winston Cup Series.

"We were lucky, and I really believe we had some help from a pretty high source," Earnhardt speculated. "You can prepare as carefully as possible and run as hard as you can, but in the end having faith and believing counts for an awful lot."

Left: Road course competition often poses a problem for NASCAR drivers accustomed to the rule "go fast, turn left." The addition of right turns and the art of subtle braking require practice to master, and here Earnhardt hones his skills at Road Atlanta.

PEAKS AND VALLEYS

Dale Earnhardt had sailed to the top of the NASCAR Winston Cup Series, but it had not all been smooth waters. As has been seen throughout NASCAR history, with drivers such as Darrell Waltrip and Rusty Wallace, and most recently Jeff Gordon, a significant portion of race fans take exception to the presence of a new driver arriving on the scene and finding success quickly at the expense of established veterans.

The race fans in 1980 were of two minds about Earnhardt, NASCAR's new star. Some loved his aggressive charges through the field, his determination to get to the front no matter the cost. Others decried what they considered to be graceless, heavy-handed tactics that amounted to nothing more than bullying. Many fans with the latter opinion were followers of Cale Yarborough, who had staged the most dogged battles with Earnhardt's number 2 Osterlund cars.

But whether or not fans agreed with Dale Earnhardt's tactics or driving style, there was no denying that he had become a major force, creating a lasting impact on the history of the sport in just two seasons. The fans, the media, and the other Winston Cup drivers wondered what would happen in 1981.

Earnhardt himself planned on starting off 1981 with a win in the Daytona 500. But first, there was a major change in the Winston Cup Series that Dale and all the other drivers would have to confront.

With the Detroit automakers migrating to smaller production automobiles, NASCAR felt that it had no choice but to follow suit. In 1981, the wheelbases of the racing stock cars shrank from 115 to 110 inches (292.1 to 279.4cm). It may seem like a minor change, but at two hundred mph (321.8kph) on a superspeedway like Daytona, such a seemingly insignificant change can easily disrupt the delicate balance between horsepower and aerodynamics, sometimes with disastrous consequences.

One of the first drivers to test the new size of Winston Cup racing was Bobby Allison. "The car is not handling well at all," the veteran driver reported. "After two days of testing, all we did was get the car from horrible to bad."

When Earnhardt had his chance at a Daytona test session, his report was no less optimistic.

"I was nervous as hell during those tests," Dale stated. "The cars aren't stable enough to run in a pack."

Earnhardt nervous? Fans knew the situation must have really been bad. But one thing about NASCAR's rules: they generally put everyone at the same disadvantage. The drivers and teams of the Winston Cup Series would have to adapt and go on.

Opposite: In late September 1980, a smiling Dale Earnhardt, his jumpsuit sporting hardly any advertisements at all, contemplates the possibility of becoming the Winston Cup champion in only his second year of competition.

Earnhardt would be going on with a bold new look for his cars. Osterlund's team had secured sponsorship from Wrangler, the jeans clothing company, and Dale's car featured a bright yellow front half, with "Jeans Machine" emblazoned across the car's blue rear.

The new paint scheme debuted at the season's first race, the road event in Riverside, California. Dale sped to a third-place finish, then negotiated the tricky aerodynamics of his downsized Pontiac stock car to take home a fifth-place finish at the Daytona 500. A top-ten at Richmond followed. Dale Earnhardt was well on his way to contending for a second consecutive NASCAR Winston Cup Series title.

But it was not to be.

Racing is as much a sport of personal chemistry as it is of speed and courage. The interplay of a team, from the owner to the crew chief to the driver to the crew, works best when everyone is focused on succeeding on the track. External distractions can be fatal to a championship quest. In 1981, the Osterlund team found itself facing the most unsettling of distractions.

By May, rumors were circulating through the garage area that Osterlund, a real estate businessman, was in severe financial trouble. Supposedly the team was for sale. So prevalent was the speculation that Rod Osterlund himself felt the need to issue a

public statement denying that the team was for sale. Two weeks later Osterlund sold the team to the mercurial J.D. Stacy.

Personnel upheavals followed, leading Earnhardt himself to quit the team the day after finishing twenty-ninth at the August race at Talladega Superspeedway in Alabama.

Richard Childress was an experienced NASCAR Winston Cup driver, but in more than a decade of competing in the top stock car circuit, his best finish was a third-place, one of just six top-five finishes. Childress wanted to build a successful and competitive team, and when Earnhardt became available, he saw his chance. Childress retired from driving on the spot and hired Dale to finish out the season. Six of Dale's crew members from the Osterlund team went with him.

"It's just like starting a new job," Childress said at the time. "I'm looking forward to my new position. Campaigning a competitive team has always been my goal.

"I just never thought that I would get a driver of Dale Earnhardt's capabilities and a sponsor like Wrangler."

Earnhardt managed six top-ten finishes while driving for Childress in the last eleven events of the season, but he had fallen to seventh in the points standings by the time the season ended. Darrell Waltrip was crowned champion.

Though Earnhardt had been able to maintain a respectable presence in Winston Cup competition while driving for Childress, both men knew the team was not one of the sport's elite organizations.

Opposite: Having won the 1980 championship, everything seemed to be going Dale Earnhardt's way. But a team ownership change would make the 1981 season a chaotic one for the defending champion.

The two parted ways on good terms. For 1982, Dale Earnhardt would be driving a Ford for Bud Moore, whose team was based in South Carolina.

Moore, a highly decorated Word War II veteran, was a longtime builder of Ford racing machines and one of the most respected names in NASCAR. In 1981, Benny Parsons had driven Moore's cars to three victories and seven more top-fives. Earnhardt felt he had a good chance to win big while teamed with Moore.

It took until April of the 1982 season, but Dale Earnhardt finally battled his way back to victory lane. It happened at Darlington International Raceway in South Carolina, the historic track that drivers feel is among the toughest. Dale, holding off Cale Yarborough, won in his Thunderbird by less than a car length.

"I knew we had Cale beat when I glanced to the left and didn't see anything at the flag stand," the jubilant Earnhardt said. "We knew we could win if the car would just stay together."

Earnhardt felt renewed momentum, and even a devastating end-over-end crash at Pocono International Raceway couldn't keep him out of the cockpit. Earnhardt's broken left knee was surgically repaired, and the tough competitor didn't miss one race on the schedule.

Though Dale had found his way back to the winner's circle, consistency was a problem for the team. When the season drew to a close, Dale had fallen to twelfth in the points standings.

The Riverside race had been moved on the schedule to close the season, so Earnhardt and the Moore team looked to Daytona to get 1983 off to a

winning start. But sixty-three laps into the event, the car suffered engine failure. Earnhardt walked away with a disappointing thirty-fifth place finish.

It was an up-and-down beginning to the season: they ran second at Richmond and thirty-third at Rockingham and Atlanta. Truth be told, there were more downs than ups, as bad finishes plagued the team throughout the spring.

Finally, though, the month of May brought a return of the top-ten finishes that Earnhardt had become accustomed to. In July, he took Moore's Ford back to victory lane, passing Neil Bonnett and powering on to win in Nashville. Two weeks later, going from short tracks to superspeedways, Earnhardt blew past Darrell Waltrip with the help of drafting partner Bobby Allison to win again on the last lap at Talladega.

"He helped me a little by pushing me past Darrell," Earnhardt admitted. "I don't think I could have gotten by before the corner without him, but I think I would have gotten past him on down in the corner."

Though the winning had returned, and Dale would finish the season an improved eighth in the points, in October word broke that Dale Earnhardt would be leaving the Moore team.

Opposite: Teamed with legendary car owner Bud Moore in 1982, Earnhardt tries his hand with a Ford Motor Company product. Note the boxy profile of this car, a far cry from the sleek Taurus model that Ford drivers compete in today.

Above: The intensity of a winner. Earnhardt's fierce determination helped him conquer NASCAR's toughest series.

"As far as I'm concerned, Dale is through with us," Bud Moore told *The Charlotte Observer* a little later in the season.

"A good while back, we both agreed that Dale would give me a decision by five o'clock on October 17 on whether he was staying or leaving to join another team. But I haven't heard from him since last Thursday, when he called to say he'd be down on Friday to talk things over.

"I have to assume, then, that he's leaving."

LAYING A FOUNDATION

In 1981, when Dale Earnhardt left his championship team, which had just been sold by Rod Osterlund, driver Richard Childress had practically leapt from the driver's seat to make room for Earnhardt to compete for his team. And even though Dale had moved on to race Fords for NASCAR legend Bud Moore in 1982 and 1983, Earnhardt and Childress had parted as friends and kept in contact within the confines of the Winston Cup garage area.

Richard Childress, born on September 21, 1945, was like Dale Earnhardt, a product of North Carolina. And like Dale, Childress was fascinated early on by stock car racing. Growing up in Winston-Salem, North Carolina, his heroes were men like Tim Flock, the founders of the rough-and-tumble sport that has grown into today's modern Winston Cup Series.

After going through his teenage years following racing, even selling programs at North Carolina's historic Bowman-Grey bullring track, it was no surprise that Richard Childress would try his hand at the Grand National stock car racing he had followed for so long.

Childress' first start came in 1969, and even though he finished well outside of the top ten and completed just eighty laps, it encouraged him to try again in 1971. The young driver made twelve starts that season and fifteen the next, during years when Richard Petty claimed consecutive Winston Cup championships. Though Childress was not setting the series on fire, he pressed on.

The first sign of some success for Childress was in 1973, when he scored his first top-five finish. It

Left: Richard Childress competed in NASCAR's top series for more than a decade, beginning with his first start in 1969.

Opposite: Preparing for competition in 1978, Childress sits surrounded by the roll cage of his stock car. Within three short years, Childress would yield the driver seat to Dale Earnhardt.

came at one of NASCAR's most storied racetracks, the historic Darlington International Raceway, on April 15, 1973. The Rebel 500 of that day saw just fourteen cars from a starting field of forty still running at the end of a very tough race. And though David Pearson easily scored the win with a dominating margin, for Childress to have claimed fourth place in his Chevrolet while performing so respectably at such a legendary—and intimidating—speedway must have been incredibly rewarding.

Richard Childress' name began to slowly climb in the championship points rankings, moving from fifteenth in 1973 up to fifth in 1975.

From 1976 on, Childress earned his success on his own. Responsible for every aspect of his racing operation as both owner and driver, he was what is known as an independent, a breed almost lost to today's NASCAR Winston Cup world of multicar teams and megadollar sponsorships.

"I worked on my race car until after midnight every night during the week," Childress recalled of the demands of operating his own team, "and on Fridays we would load the car on the trailer, drive all night to the track and qualify on Saturday. On Sundays I would race for 500 miles [805km] then turn around and drive another couple hundred miles home and begin the week all over again."

The best finish of Childress' twelve-season career driving in NASCAR Winston Cup stock car racing came on July 15, 1978. Racing 250 miles (402.3km) at the tight short track in Nashville, Tennessee, Childress finished just ahead of Dave

Marcis to claim third place. More than a decade later, Childress' support would help Marcis continue his racing career as one of the last independents in NASCAR's top series.

The cars that Richard Childress had prepared for Dale Earnhardt during their brief alliance in 1981 performed relatively well, with Dale racing to two top-five finishes and a handful of top-tens. After Dale departed for Bud Moore's South Carolina-based racing operation, Childress decided to stay in the pits and signed another young driver, Virginia's Ricky Rudd.

Ricky Rudd was twenty-six years old when he joined Childress for the 1982 season. Most of his starts had come at the wheel of a team operated by his father, Al. But in 1981, Rudd had climbed to sixth in the Winston Cup points while driving Buicks and Chevrolets for Bill Gardiner. The opportunity to team his talent with Childress' experience had considerable potential.

The Childress team claimed two poles and finished second twice in their first year with Rudd at the wheel of the team's Chevrolets; they took a total of six top-fives. Clearly, they were poised to win in 1983.

The first victory for the Richard Childress team came on June 5, 1983. The Winston Cup cars had journeyed to the West Coast to race at the fast, 2.5-

mile (4.02km) road course at Riverside International Raceway. Rudd had qualified the Piedmont-sponsored Childress car well, starting the day in the fourth position. Rudd recovered from running off the course to avoid an accident halfway through the event, and he charged on to take the lead with forty laps remaining. He tenaciously clung to first place and delivered Childress' first win, outpacing runner-up Bill Elliott. Dale Earnhardt drove Moore's Ford to fourth place.

In late September, Rudd won for the Childress team again, this time at the demanding short track in Martinsville, Virginia, beating Bobby Allison to the checkered flag. Earnhardt again finished in fourth place.

At the end of the season, Rudd appeared poised to move to the RahMoc racing team, but a deal was engineered by Winston Cup sponsor Wrangler Jeans to bring Rudd to Bud Moore's team. In the wake of Dale Earnhardt's plans to depart Moore's operation, Wrangler agreed to sponsor both Earnhardt and whomever would drive for Moore in 1984. Wrangler was impressed with Rudd's runs for Childress, so for the upcoming season the company's blue-and-yellow colors would be flown on both Moore's Fords with Rudd driving, and Childress' Chevrolets with Earnhardt behind the wheel.

In the end, the deal-making amounted to a swap of rides for Ricky Rudd and Dale Earnhardt, but the switch created a union between Earnhardt and Richard Childress that would strike fear in the hearts of the other teams competing in the Winston Cup Series.

Opposite: Though he tried year after year, Richard Childress just couldn't pull out a victory in NASCAR's top series as a driver.

Above: As a car owner, however, Childress often found his way to victory lane once he'd handed the steering wheel to Dale Earnhardt. Here the two men celebrate a win at Martinsville in 1991.

VICTORY

WRANGLING VICTORY LANE

A thrilling, talented driver with nine victories in his young career. A car owner who had turned his team around, winning twice in the most recent season. The Winston Cup world waited to see what would happen when these two men, Dale Earnhardt and Richard Childress, joined forces to build on a wealth of winning experience.

NASCAR fans also cast an interested eye toward the alliance of Bud Moore and driver Ricky Rudd, to see how the "driver trade of 1983" would play out over the course of the 1984 season and beyond.

The first indications of the season came, as always, at the Daytona 500. Cale Yarborough won his second straight edition of The Great American Race, sling-shotting his Chevrolet past rival Darrell Waltrip on the final lap. Following Cale through was Dale Earnhardt, who scored his best finish to date in the 500 when he grabbed second, leaving Waltrip to settle for third.

But a week later, all eyes turned to Rudd at the wheel of Moore's Ford. From the huge superspeedway at Daytona, the Winston Cup Series had

Pages 36–37: Throughout the mid-1980s and beyond, the awesome pit crew of the Richard Childress Racing team helped Dale win race after race.

Right: At Bristol International Raceway on April 1, 1979, a beaming Dale Earnhardt clutches his first Winston Cup trophy. It was the first in a long line of victories that he would claim on his way to becoming one of the greatest drivers in NASCAR's history.

journeyed to the tight half-mile at Richmond Fairgrounds Raceway in Virginia. Rudd, a native of Virginia, always seemed to perform well in his home state. This race was no exception. Rudd had just survived a terrible crash at Daytona, but he fought off any lingering effects of the accident while fighting off Darrell Waltrip for the win at Richmond.

Some in the Winston Cup garage area began to wonder if perhaps Moore hadn't got the better part of the deal in the Earnhardt-Rudd swap. Dale himself addressed the issue days later in an interview with Tom Higgins of *The Charlotte Observer*.

"I think in the long run the moves that we made will prove equally good for both me and Ricky," Earnhardt insisted. "And I'm not saying that to be diplomatic. I really believe it.

"In the meantime, I still say and feel what I have all along—that if I'm going to win another Grand National championship this year, or anytime soon, I had better get back in a Chevy to do it. Why? The Chevys are just better cars if you're going to chase the championship. You have to be consistent to win the title and consistency seems to be one of the strong advantages of the Chevrolets."

Asked about Rudd's trip to victory lane so early in the new season, Earnhardt was adamant that he had made the right choice in moving back to the Childress team.

"Right now, I guess most folks would figure that Ricky is up on us because he has won this year and we haven't," Dale admitted. "Even so, I'd still do it over again, definitely. I don't think there has been a time in my career when I've felt any better

about a situation or been any more optimistic than I am now.

"I honestly think that me and Richard and the boys are ready to fire on 'em. We're running better and better each time out and we've got some tracks where I normally do pretty well coming up on the schedule."

Earnhardt backed up his prediction by finishing second at Atlanta, crossing the finish line less than a second behind winner Benny Parsons. He followed that up with consecutive top-tens at Bristol International Speedway, North Wilkesboro Speedway, Darlington Raceway, and Martinsville Speedway.

The Childress team was picking up momentum, and Earnhardt was pounding on the door of victory lane. He finished second in the grueling six-hundred-mile (965.4km) race at Charlotte Motor Speedway, fifth at Riverside, eighth at Pocono, and second again at Michigan International Speedway.

Though the strong runs of Earnhardt were impressive, all eyes in Winston Cup racing were on The King, Richard Petty, as NASCAR arrived at Daytona International Speedway on July 4. Petty was seeking an unprecedented two-hundredth Winston Cup victory, and President Ronald Reagan journeyed down to the 2.5-mile (4.02km) super-speedway to see if Petty could do it on America's birthday. In a thrilling battle to a late-race caution flag that would determine the race winner, Petty held off Cale Yarborough's aggressive charge to notch win two hundred.

More important to Dale Earnhardt, though, was the fact that his eighth-place finish put him in

Right: His blue-and-yellow Chevrolet in victory lane again, Earnhardt smiles after conquering the field in a 500-mile (800km) race at Atlanta in 1986. The trophy Dale clutches says it all: "winner."

the lead of the championship battle, by forty points over Darrell Waltrip.

The consistency finally paid off later in the month, at the intimidating Alabama International Motor Speedway in Talladega (now known as Talladega Superspeedway). Known for close competition and even closer finishes, a battle among ten cars for the win sent NASCAR officials off to review photographic evidence to determine exactly who finished where. Despite pressure from Terry Labonte and Buddy Baker, there was no doubt about which car crossed the finish line first: the blue-and-yellow Chevrolet of Dale Earnhardt.

"This is the greatest race I've ever been involved in," Dale enthused after the win. "When I got by Terry, I looked in my mirror and saw him and Buddy running side-by-side. I knew I had it won then."

Dale took the opportunity to address those who suggested his driving in 1984 was less aggressive than it needed to be, that he was, in racing slang, "stroking."

"Just because I hadn't won this year, they were taking shots at me. I'd finished second four times, right on the bumper of the winners almost, and I

was supposed to be stroking. Now that doesn't make sense."

A second win for the Richard Childress team came late in the year, at Atlanta International Raceway, when Earnhardt held off Bill Elliott's challenge.

Dale closed 1984 fourth in the points, as Terry Labonte was crowned NASCAR Winston Cup champion for the first time. Harry Gant and Bill

Elliott had also finished ahead of the Childress team. Still, it was an encouraging start to the reunion, and the Bud Moore/Ricky Rudd team finished three spots in the points behind Earnhardt.

Though Bill Elliott won the Daytona 500—his first trip to victory lane in a season that saw Awesome Bill score an astonishing eleven wins—Dale Earnhardt found his winning ways for 1985 the next week at Richmond.

▰▰▰▰▰▰▰▰▰▰▰▰▰▰▰▰▰▰▰▰▰▰▰▰▰▰▰▰▰▰▰▰▰▰

Above: At Darlington in 1985, Terry Labonte looks in his rearview mirror and sees one of the most fearsome sights in NASCAR racing: Dale Earnhardt closing in.

Opposite: A large part of the success claimed by the Childress team was due to the painstaking preparation of the Chevrolets driven by Dale Earnhardt. All the hard work and long hours put in here at the race shop paid off in a big way for the whole team.

A master of short-track racing, where skill and aggression are required in equal measure, Earnhardt had to rub his way past Tim Richmond to get to the front. The sight of Earnhardt trading paint with his competitors was loved by many Winston Cup fans, despised by others.

"That's just racing," Earnhardt said of his battle for the win with Richmond. "I think he'd try to do the same thing. Anybody would. If they say they wouldn't, they're lying. We're all out there to win."

But it's not just the other drivers a Winston Cup competitor must deal with. Sometimes his own stock car presents a driver with obstacles that are even more daunting. That was the case at Bristol, where Dale's power steering failed just one hundred laps into the five-hundred-lap event. Wrestling the heavy stock car around the tight track at speeds of more than 130 mph (209.2kph), Earnhardt used every bit of his strength to win his second race of the year.

In August, Earnhardt used the physical approach to passing in order to win at Bristol again, and the victim for the second time that year was Tim Richmond.

"He used one of his normal tactics," Richmond said of Dale's charge. "But I'm not mad. It was good, hard racing, and I knew what to expect from him."

Earnhardt won his fourth race of the year at Martinsville, completing a season in which he excelled on the short tracks.

Though the Childress team had neatly doubled its win total from 1984, as far as the championship points standings were concerned, 1985 was a step back. Dale Earnhardt finished eighth in the standings, more than seven hundred points behind champion Darrell Waltrip.

Winning the Winston Cup championship requires the right balance of hard charging and consistency. The points system turns a favorable eye toward regular top-five and top-ten finishes. Winning the most races does not guarantee a championship, as Bill Elliott found out in 1985. With that in mind, Earnhardt and his Childress team turned toward the 1986 season.

Dale was a top contender in the Daytona 500, ready to battle Geoff Bodine for the victory, when his Chevrolet faltered; it had run out of gas. The late-race pit stop cost Earnhardt dearly, and his number 3 car came home in a disappointing fourteenth place. But the real fireworks were yet to come.

Earnhardt pulled into the second race of the season as a defending-event champion at Richmond Fairgrounds Raceway. He was determined to win the race again and make up for Daytona—no matter

what the cost, his critics might add. No matter where fault is placed, there is no doubt about one thing: the Miller High Life 400 was one wild race.

Above: The Richard Childress Racing brain trust ponders what to do to get Dale into victory lane at Daytona in 1987. The somber looks on the faces of (left to right) Earnhardt, Childress, and crew chief Kirk Shelmerdine indicate all was not right with the Monte Carlo's performance on the superspeedway.

Earnhardt had shown that he might be the class of the field by running up front all day. Darrell Waltrip had other ideas about who should be leading. With three laps to go, Waltrip powered his Junior Johnson-owned Chevrolet past Earnhardt and into the lead on the backstretch. Dale took exception to the idea of giving up first place and made his move trying to get around Waltrip. But Earnhardt's front end made solid contact with

Darrell's rear quarter panel, and the wreck was on. When it was over, Earnhardt, Waltrip, Geoff Bodine, and Joe Ruttman—the drivers running in first through fourth positions—were all caught up in the crash. The only person happy about the turn of events was Kyle Petty, who had been cruising along well behind the others in fifth. He could hardly believe his luck when everyone in front of him crashed, allowing him to inherit first place and claim his first Winston Cup Series victory.

NASCAR immediately moved to penalize Earnhardt for setting off the disaster. There were many in the Winston Cup garage who thought it was about time Dale was reprimanded for what they considered to be overly aggressive driving.

"I haven't ever had a run-in with Earnhardt before," Waltrip said after the race. "Everyone else has and he's not choosy. He turned left into me. I want to win as much as anybody, but I've never tried to hurt anyone."

Waltrip's car owner, Junior Johnson, himself a retired driver (whom some consider the greatest ever)—and one of the most aggressive ever—insisted that Earnhardt's actions "were no different than if he had put a loaded gun to Darrell's head and pulled the trigger."

NASCAR fined Earnhardt five thousand dollars, placed him on a year's probation, and demanded he post a ten-thousand-dollar bond to continue competing on the circuit.

"I think the fine line was violated when Earnhardt hit Darrell," said Geoff Bodine, who found himself a victim of the tangle. "I think

NASCAR made a good decision. We'll see how much good it does. Something has got to be done to stop some of the things which have been going on. We're lucky nobody has been hurt."

"I was trying to dive under him in the third turn," Earnhardt insisted in his defense. "I barely clipped him in the rear end and spun us both. I wasn't trying to wreck him. If I was, I wouldn't have wrecked myself, that's for damn sure."

Eventually the fine was reduced and the probation and bond requirement lifted, partially on the strength of a letter of support for Earnhardt signed by others in Winston Cup racing, including Ricky Rudd. No matter what, the incident and the controversy that followed helped attract attention to the sport and to Dale Earnhardt. And those who watched him race, with renewed enthusiasm or abundant dislike, witnessed Dale carving a path to the top of the Winston Cup points chase.

After falling just short to Morgan Shepherd at Atlanta, Dale won for the first time in 1986 at historic Darlington Raceway. Known as the "track too tough to tame," the egg-shaped superspeedway is held in highest esteem by drivers. Winning there is an undeniable proof of talent, and Earnhardt dominated, leading all but thirty-two laps.

"We had 'em covered today," Dale said.

On a roll, Earnhardt won the next event, at North Wilkesboro, and after suffering uncharacteristic motor problems at Martinsville, he assumed the points lead by finishing second at Talladega. It was a lead he would not relinquish for the rest of the season.

The Monster Mile in Dover, Delaware, gave Dale a third-place finish, and Earnhardt then moved on to Charlotte for the six-hundred-mile (965.4km) race. When Bill Elliott was forced to surrender the lead to take on fuel late in the race, Earnhardt was in position to win. He held off Tim Richmond and won by almost two seconds.

"The track came to me," Dale explained. "It was cloudy earlier and when the sun came out our car started working better."

As the season wore on, it became clear that the two contenders for the Winston Cup championship were Dale Earnhardt and Darrell Waltrip. In classic

To prove his point, Earnhardt hammered out another win at Charlotte Motor Speedway, coming from two laps down to take the victory. Waltrip had to settle for ninth. Dale headed into the last three races of the season with a 159-point advantage over his nemesis.

As it turned out, Dale needed just two of those races to sew up the championship. Though Waltrip put on the pressure with a third-place run at Rockingham, besting Dale's sixth-place finish, Earnhardt retaliated by winning at Atlanta International Raceway. Waltrip had fallen from the race on lap eighty-three with engine problems, and his title hopes were dashed.

Six years after stunning the NASCAR world with consecutive Rookie of the Year and championship seasons, Dale Earnhardt had locked down his second Winston Cup Series championship. The 1986 season had been an impressive one for Richard Childress Racing, the five victories providing the foundation for sixteen top-fives and twenty-three top-tens. That is the kind of consistency that wins championships.

"I'm not going to compare the two titles, but this one means an awful lot because of the dedication of the boys on my crew and Richard Childress," a grateful Dale Earnhardt said after the championship was his. "Richard was our key to winning the championship. His effort as team owner put us where we are. All the glory is his."

fashion, the verbal sparring approached the intensity of the action on the track.

After winning at North Wilkesboro, Waltrip announced that he had considered "putting some psychological stuff in the papers, but it wouldn't do any good because Dale and his boys can't read."

Never one to shy away, Earnhardt shot back: "I can read. Just like in a kid's early reader. See Darrell run his mouth. See Darrell fall."

DOMINATION

It had begun as a dream of following in his father's footsteps, but with his second championship in 1986, it was clear in the world of racing that Dale Earnhardt had already reached heights that father Ralph Earnhardt had only been able to dream of attaining.

Winning a championship is one thing; defending it is another. Years had passed between Earnhardt's first two titles, but with the Richard Childress Racing team firing on all cylinders, Earnhardt was determined to start up in 1987 where he had left off.

Dale managed to put the yellow-and-blue Wrangler Monte Carlo into the lead draft and then, briefly, into first place at Daytona, but he had to settle for a (decent) sixth-place finish. But beginning with the season's second race, things began to fall solidly into place.

At North Carolina Motor Speedway, Earnhardt assumed the lead in the last third of the race and dominated the event. His victory was assured when the race's other strongest car, driven by Neil Bonnett, had problems on a pit stop and fell a lap off the pace. Ricky Rudd finished a distant second, eleven seconds behind the streaking Earnhardt. Dale left the race tied for the points lead with Bill Elliott.

Earnhardt qualified third for the next race, at Richmond, but then one of the greatest fears of a top qualifier became a reality for Dale: he wrecked his car during practice. Under NASCAR rules, racing a backup car requires starting at the rear of the field. With track position so critical at a short track

like Richmond, starting in the rear loomed as a potential disaster.

But Earnhardt's crew came to the rescue. The Childress team rebuilt the heavily damaged stock car, and Dale was able to start the race in third position. He finished in first. Along the way, Earnhardt had contact with Harry Gant, who was far from pleased after the race.

"Earnhardt is blind as a bat," fumed Handsome Harry. "He ran all over me. He's done that before, though. It's not really a surprise when something like this happens when you run close to him. The only thing I regret is that I'm not going to get a chance to get even with him."

Again the specter of "rough driving" hung over the Childress camp, but there was no time to dwell on the hurt feelings of other drivers. Earnhardt was too busy winning races.

"Obviously I can't say enough about my crew," Earnhardt said of his team's effort to rebuild the car that won the Richmond race. "What a job! The car essentially was totaled out. Not only did they have to put a new engine and front suspension in, they had to put the car on a frame machine, a difficult deal.

"I didn't know what the car was going to do, but they assured me it was going to be all right. They were right, and I can't say enough for them. They put the car back together, and I put my trust in their promising it was OK and went out there and ran it hard."

The hard running was far from over. After qualifying on the pole but suffering electrical problems

at Atlanta, Earnhardt drove to another win at Darlington. His chief rival in the points race, Bill Elliott, seemed to have the race in hand. But Elliott's team had rolled the dice, seeking to stretch fuel mileage. The Thunderbird ran dry on the last lap.

As at Richmond, Earnhardt started the North Wilkesboro race third, and again he won. His car

Above: In 1990, Earnhardt makes an outside move on a rising young star, Alan Kulwicki. Although Kulwicki's self-owned team had financial resources that fell far short of Dale's Childress operation, Alan would eventually win the 1992 championship.

Pages 48–49: Dale Earnhardt (pitting here at Dover in 1989) is one of the lucky NASCAR drivers to have been blessed with a top-flight pit crew at every stage of his career.

was the class of the field, and the victory gave Dale a 117-point lead over Elliott.

"I know we've got an awful good team," Earnhardt said, "but it amazes me that our cars and the crew can be so consistent. If I keep my head screwed on, we're going to have a great season. It'd be great to win 12 to 15, and we're shooting for that."

An optimistic prediction, but there was no one in the Winston Cup garage area who doubted that it just might come true. After all, Earnhardt had already won four of the season's first six races—and he won again the next week at Bristol.

"This is Bristol," Earnhardt said after the win. "You've got to be aggressive to race here."

Aggression was the key word, as Dale was involved in several contact incidents. The most obvious came when he tagged race leader Sterling Marlin, setting off a crash that also caught Geoff Bodine and Ken Schrader. Predictably, the fallout from the incident was immediate.

"He hit me and spun me," was Marlin's angry analysis. "I'm the leader of the race and it's my track. He has to pass me, not spin me out. The hard thing about this whole deal is that I was running damn good and I had a real chance of winning this race. That hurts even more than him spinning me out.

"Don't worry," Sterling vowed, "his day is coming and he'll get it, too."

What Earnhardt got was yet another win, his sixth in seven races, at Martinsville. And this time, "rough driving" had nothing to do with the victory. It was all chalked up to Dale's short-track mastery—and a little bit of luck.

Geoff Bodine was in position to win the race, having powered out to a five-second lead late in the race. But passing contact with the lapped car of Kyle Petty sent Bodine's Rick Hendrick-owned Chevy into a spin. Earnhardt inherited the lead and the win.

"If you don't have a little luck, you can't win races, and this one was all luck. Geoff definitely had us beat," Dale admitted.

Young Davey Allison won at Talladega, and the big news was that someone other than Earnhardt had finally clawed his way to victory lane. Dale wasn't far from another win, however, coming home in fourth. The finish gave him a 220-point lead over rival Elliott.

As the teams headed to Charlotte Motor Speedway, the tension of the points race boiled over.

In 1985, a non-points all-star race known as The Winston was born at Charlotte, to be run the week before the traditional six-hundred-mile (965.4km) points race. In 1986, Elliott won The

Winston, with Dale close behind. Now, with the same two drivers first and second in the points battle, fans expected a real shootout between the two in The Winston. They were not disappointed.

After a restart in the final segment of the three-part race, Earnhardt and Elliott battled with a ferocity that became legendary. Swapping paint and banging doors, the two drivers made contact again and again. Coming off turn four with a handful of laps remaining, hard contact sent Earnhardt skidding across the grass of Charlotte Motor Speedway's tri-oval. The Chevrolet skated across the treacherous surface at nearly two hundred mph (321.8km) and returned to the pavement. Earnhardt applied all of his skill and kept the car under control, and in the lead. He led the rest of the way.

The daring—and lucky—excursion across the no-man's-land became known as The Pass in the Grass.

The fans loved the action; NASCAR wasn't so happy. Both Earnhardt and Elliott were fined for actions taken during the non-points race.

Perhaps the furor of The Winston had nothing to do with it, but Earnhardt and Elliott both faltered in the six-hundred-mile (965.4km) race the next week. Dale quickly regrouped with top-fives at both Dover and Pocono, capped off with a top-ten at Riverside. Then it was back to victory lane, this time at Michigan, as Dale held off a late-race charge mounted by Davey Allison (one of NASCAR's brightest new stars and the son of Bobby Allison), who won the next race at Daytona.

As the season moved into its second half, the championship battle between Earnhardt and

Opposite: *Some of Earnhardt's greatest races and fiercest battles came behind the wheels of the black Monte Carlos he raced through the 1980s. And no matter what the car, Dale could master any type of track, from superspeedways to short tracks, as he showed in this race set amid North Wilkesboro Speedway's tight confines.*

Elliott continued. Dale won at Pocono; a week later Bill won at Talladega. Elliott won at Michigan, Earnhardt a week later at Bristol. But though the drivers seemed to be trading victories in the season's second half, Earnhardt's consistency in the first half had given him a commanding lead. Consecutive wins at Darlington and Richmond gave Dale an even greater margin in the points standings.

And though Bill Elliott won the twenty-seventh race of the season at North Carolina Motor Speedway, Dale's runner-up finish closed the book on the 1987 points battle. With two races still remaining, Dale Earnhardt was crowned NASCAR Winston Cup champion for a third time.

What is domination in Winston Cup racing? Earnhardt's eleven wins and twenty-one top-fives in 1987 makes a pretty good definition.

Aside from the brilliance of Dale Earnhardt's talent behind the wheel, there were any number of key components to the awesome performance of the Richard Childress Racing team. Of course, there was Richard himself, a car owner who carefully took the steps necessary to build a winning organization. There were the powerful and—equally important—reliable engines built by mechanical master Lou LaRosa. And then there was crew chief Kirk Shelmerdine.

Shelmerdine had moved to the South from the Philadelphia area, hoping to transform his love of cars and racing into a career. After breaking into the Winston Cup ranks wrenching for longtime NASCAR competitor James Hylton, the young Shelmerdine was hired by Childress to come aboard his team. The choice paid off. Shelmerdine helped mastermind many of the greatest achievements in Earnhardt's career.

At a time when innovations like wind-tunnel testing to help tweak the aerodynamics of the Winston Cup cars was becoming commonplace, Shelmerdine had the vision to know what information should and shouldn't be taken as gospel.

"The engineers try to assist," Shelmerdine said. "Their experience, though, is located strictly within the wind tunnel; all of their time and knowledge is spent there. They don't have that much on-track experience. And there are some differences—the wind tunnel is the best way we have of checking aerodynamics. But it is still the car and the ground staying still and you're moving air across it and there are some interactions that are different when you have the air sitting still—you know like a boat on the water, the air and the water are sitting still and the vehicle moves through it. There's some differences there from when the vehicle's still and you're moving air across it. So still, on the racetrack, you have to go back up everything that you did at the wind tunnel."

Car preparation was another of Shelmerdine's strengths, and he kept ample documentation of the number 3 car's performance at every racetrack. This documentation helped ensure that when the Childress Chevrolet was unloaded from its hauler at each Winston Cup Series racetrack, the car was well on its way to being dialed in for the race at hand.

"We keep probably a dozen pages' worth of data on every race, so that we can go by the last time, kind of as a baseline," Shelmerdine explained.

"Things change, like tire compounds for one thing may change from one race to the next at a given track, or the weather's different. A lot of the stuff doesn't apply then, but it's a real good baseline—especially if things went well the previous time, you can base a lot of stuff on that or use it as a starting off point. But there's a lot of maintenance on the cars between a race, so actually the preparation for a given race begins a couple or three weeks before a race for that particular car."

Above: Earnhardt steers one of the newer Chevrolet Luminas in 1990. Though the car was a change from the Monte Carlo body style, Dale's seat was still mounted low and far back—his preferred cockpit setup.

Crucial to the success of a Winston Cup team is communication, especially between a driver and his crew chief. During the races that led to the Childress team's championships, though, Shelmerdine and Earnhardt kept their radio communications to a minimum.

"Most people say we don't talk much," Shelmerdine admitted. "Sometimes the fans have scanners and they figure out what frequency we're on and they listen and they say, 'You don't say anything all day long!' Well, there isn't a whole lot to talk about except for right before we're going to have a pit stop, we'll talk about it for two or three laps, then we'll do it and then it's over with.

"Dale gives us feedback periodically on how the car's driving and if we might do something to change the handling a little bit," Shelmerdine continued, "but most of the time the driving takes extreme concentration. We just let him go do his thing and he does it. So there's not a whole lot of discussion; we try to keep it to a minimum. He doesn't like to hear his lap times or anything like that; he can tell when he's fast and when he's not."

Earnhardt was almost always fast. But in 1988, the sight of a speeding Dale Earnhardt changed from a blue-and-yellow blur to a black flash. The success of Richard Childress Racing with its Chevrolets had enticed General Motors to align itself with the winning combination. Now Goodwrench, the automotive parts and service subsidiary of GM, replaced Wrangler as Dale's sponsor. It was the beginning of a long-term relationship that would forever associate Earnhardt with ominous-looking black Chevrolets emblazoned with a large, white number 3.

Earnhardt first won for his new sponsor at the fourth race of the 1988 season, in a dominating performance both on the track and in the pits at Atlanta International Raceway.

"It was a team victory," Dale said after the race. "The car was perfect, but the pit crew was better than perfect. They can change four tires quicker than most other crews change two."

Earnhardt won again at Martinsville in April, once again showing off his brilliant short-track skills. But then a victory drought began that would last until late August.

Though Earnhardt won the traditional night race at Bristol International Raceway, his customary lead in the Winston Cup points at this stage in the season was nowhere to be seen. As the teams left Bristol's tight high banks, it was Earnhardt's long-time rival Bill Elliott who led the points race, having taken the lead from Rusty Wallace.

Dale's three victories in the season weren't enough, as Wallace and Elliott racked up six apiece. Elliott was crowned champion by a handful of points over Wallace; Earnhardt was third, more than two hundred points behind his fellow competitors.

The Childress team knew it had to improve its performances in 1989, and it did just that.

Earnhardt struck first at North Wilkesboro in April, in a race that found many drivers uneasy over Goodyear's introduction of a new element in Winston Cup racing: radial tires. Earnhardt felt comfortable enough though, winning by three seconds over Alan Kulwicki.

In June, Earnhardt finally found triumph at one of the few racetracks whose victory lane had yet to host him. Dover Downs International Speedway was considered a track where Fords always performed well; not on this day.

"All I'd heard all week was 'Ford track, Ford track,'" Earnhardt commented. "Well, a racetrack is a racetrack and a race car is a race car. There ain't no Ford track, Chevrolet track, or Chrysler track in the world, and today proves it."

Earnhardt drove to his Dover conquest at the wheel of a new Chevrolet Lumina. After a distinguished career in the Winston Cup Series, the Monte Carlo was being retired from Chevrolet's stock car program in favor of the superior aerodynamics of the new Lumina.

Dale used those aerodynamics to his advantage Labor Day Weekend, beating Mark Martin by more than a second to win the Southern 500 at Darlington. The weekend was special for another reason as well: Dale's father, Ralph Earnhardt, was inducted into the Stock Car Racing Hall of Fame, one of the sport's greatest honors.

Earnhardt swept the Dover races by winning the second race of the season, held at The Monster

Below: A frustrated Earnhardt looks on as his crew struggles to repair the damaged number 3 during the 1990 season. Though Earnhardt's cars often returned to the garage worse for wear, it was rare to see Dale fall out of competition before the checkered flag waved.

Mile. More importantly, he closed ground in the championship points race, an all-out battle that also included Rusty Wallace, Mark Martin, Darrell Waltrip, Ken Schrader, and Bill Elliott.

It came down to the last race of the season. Dale Earnhardt did all he could do at Atlanta, hammering out a spectacular win by a margin of more than twenty-five seconds over Geoff Bodine. But Rusty Wallace, by finishing in fifteenth place, scored just enough points to beat Earnhardt for the championship. The margin was incredibly slim: twelve points. Never again would race fans wonder why drivers fight for every chance at moving up even one position when points are awarded.

Despite losing the title by such a frustrating amount, Earnhardt had reason for optimism as the 1990 season dawned. In 1989, he had gone from three wins to six. Could he go from six to nine?

Earnhardt fought off illness for his first win of the year, at Atlanta. Darlington may be known as "too tough to tame," but it wasn't for Earnhardt. He followed up his win in the 1989 Southern 500 with another victory at the track in April. Then it was on to the huge superspeedway at Talladega, where Earnhardt used his Lumina's aerodynamics to carve out a win that gave him a ninety-point lead in the season championship race.

The team encountered problems in several races but straightened things out when Dale beat Ernie Irvan at Michigan in June. Mark Martin had assumed the points lead, but Earnhardt sensed his opportunity to close in. He bore down, winning the next race—Daytona's four-hundred-mile (643.6km)

event. Later in the month, it was Dale in victory lane again at Talladega. The Intimidator had cut Martin's lead down to a single point.

Though Ernie Irvan had won his first Winston Cup race at Bristol the week before, at Darlington Earnhardt beat Irvan again, as he had done at Michigan weeks earlier. Dale was continuing to demonstrate his brilliance at facing the challenge of Darlington, and the victory was his second consecutive Southern 500.

"I had to work hard today," Earnhardt said. "Any time you race at Darlington, it's tough. Add the heat and it's tougher. There are so many things here. You have to be careful. You can't ever forget where you're racing when you're racing here. When I got out of that car, I felt like I had run 100 laps on foot."

But Mark Martin had been running strong as well, and despite winning at Darlington, Dale was twenty-six points behind Martin as the season wore on.

Determined to claim the championship again, Earnhardt drove strong and won at Richmond. That closed the points margin, but not by much. Martin finished the race in second, just feet behind Earnhardt.

At Dover, Bill Elliott scored a win, but Martin and Earnhardt were in second and third, respectively. A similar scenario unfolded at Martinsville, as Geoff Bodine won, but Earnhardt came in second and Martin in third. Martin won at North Wilkesboro, but it didn't do him much good. Earnhardt finished second.

It was a fantastic championship battle, pitting a NASCAR veteran against a newcomer, a Chevrolet against a Ford. It was no surprise that it all came down to the last race of the season.

Earnhardt had won at Phoenix and clung to a six-point lead over Martin as the teams assembled at Atlanta International Raceway to settle the 1990 championship struggle. Martin arrived at Atlanta under curious circumstances. Rather than drive one of the Jack Roush Thunderbirds he had competed in all season, Martin and the Roush team elected to race in a Ford built by Robert Yates for his driver, Davey Allison. It was an attempt by the Ford teams to pool their talent and resources. The mission: stop Earnhardt and his Chevrolet.

The mission failed.

Dale Earnhardt finished the race in third; the best Martin could coax from his Yates mount was sixth. For the fourth time in his career, Dale Earnhardt was the NASCAR Winston Cup champion.

"It's been a tough year, really," Earnhardt said after Martin's challenge had been turned back. "We've won races, but we got behind in the points. It's a hard fight to come back from where we did. I can't say enough for the team."

From three wins in 1988, to six wins in 1989, to nine wins in 1990. With that kind of improvement and four championships already in hand, people began to wonder if Earnhardt might not have a chance at reaching Richard Petty's all-time NASCAR record of seven championships.

"Three more is a long way off, way out there," Dale pointed out. "I feel at age thirty-nine I've got

ten more competitive years of driving left, so I might get that many. But even if I do, Richard Petty is way away from anything I could be. He's The King, and it'd make me proud to do something only he has done."

Above: In 1990, Earnhardt had reason to smile. He was the most feared of all Winston Cup competitors, drove the fastest and best-prepared stock cars, and had the fastest pit crew around.

A LEGEND OF

REACHING FOR ROYALTY

After the 1990 season, many observers of stock car racing, from fans to media, spent the off-season debating if Dale Earnhardt's mastery of the Winston Cup Series had positioned him within striking distance of King Richard Petty's record of seven NASCAR championships.

But many of the competitors in NASCAR's elite division faced a more immediate problem: how to stop Earnhardt on a race-by-race basis.

"It makes me feel good to hear that other teams think they have to beat us to win the championship," said Earnhardt before the season's first green flag waved. "I'm glad they're talking about us that way. If that's intimidation and it gives us a little edge, we'll take it."

While some teams tried to come up with novel approaches to improve their performance—within the rules or not—to stop the "3 car" team, the Childress organization concentrated on fundamentals.

"There are so many areas that need attention, that just, if done correctly, will be such an advantage that you don't have to spend all your time on stuff that's not kosher," crew chief Kirk Shelmerdine emphatically stated. "There are so many things that are wrong, such as procedure management things, and just within the guidelines you can just do them correctly and be so far ahead of the game that it's not even funny. That's the kind of thing that we've concentrated on over the years. All we were doing was kind of taking a look at everything and doing everything correctly. There are so many people that are off in left [field] doing crazy stuff that they're missing the little things that are really the bread and butter stuff anyway. We just stuck with that kind of thing. It was surprising to us but we made a lot of headway by doing that."

Following and refining this back-to-basics approach, Earnhardt won his first race of 1991 at the second event of the schedule. A heated battle with Ricky Rudd resulted in Earnhardt nipping the Virginia driver for the victory. The next trip to the winner's circle came just weeks later at Martinsville.

From the short tracks to the superspeedways, Earnhardt showed he could conquer them all. Having won at two of the half-mile tracks, Dale next won at Talladega in July, the largest and fastest of the NASCAR superspeedways. Though the Fords of Bill Elliott and Mark Martin made a furious charge at Earnhardt's black Lumina, Dale hung on, first drafting with Ricky Rudd and then using his experience to do whatever was necessary to win.

"I was watching behind me as much as in front of me," Earnhardt recalled. "Ricky and I were trying to work together. I looked up and saw those

Pages 60–61: Dale Earnhardt prepares to race. Although many Winston Cup drivers use fully enclosed helmets, Earnhardt prefered the old-fashioned open face models.

Opposite: Dale's early reputation was built on the ovals of the Winston Cup Series, but as his career progressed, he also mastered the road courses, including this one at Sears Point, California.

Fords coming. When they passed Ricky, I knew I had to work them. I dropped low to block them, and that broke the draft with Ricky. I hated to do that, but I had to look after myself."

Perhaps Dale didn't mind quite so much that Rudd fell from contention for the win. After all, Earnhardt left Talladega with a 160-point lead over his nearest championship challenger: Ricky Rudd.

As the season moved into fall, the talk of the series was the incredible winning streak Harry Gant had embarked upon. Picking up the nickname Mr. September, Gant had won four Winston Cup races in a row. Would it be five?

Gant may have had a streak to continue, but Earnhardt had a championship to win. When Handsome Harry had late-race braking problems, Earnhardt passed him with nine laps left and moved into the lead. Gant's streak was over, but Dale's championship drive was alive and well.

Though the Richard Childress Racing team had suffered a drop-off in the win column, its strong runs gave Earnhardt such a commanding points lead that he wrapped up the 1991 Winston Cup championship at Phoenix International Raceway, with the season's final race still to be run in Atlanta.

"We wanted to wrap it up here. Richard Childress might just lock me up to make sure I get to Atlanta," the five-time champion joked. "I've got a lot of deer hunting to do. If I don't fall out of a tree, we'll be all right."

With back-to-back championships in hand, speculation about Earnhardt's chances of reaching—or even surpassing—Petty's record seven titles grew. And the possibility of Dale claiming three championships in a row seemed very real.

The possibility of such a streak faded as the new year unfolded. The 1992 season was an uncharacteristic one for Richard Childress Racing. Poor performances, ranging from mechanical failures to just plain bad luck, plagued the team. In 1991, Earnhardt had four wins, fourteen top-fives, and twenty-one top-tens on the way to the championship. But 1992 yielded just six top-fives and fifteen top-tens. The only victory of the season came in the six-hundred-mile (965.4km) race at Charlotte Motor Speedway. Earnhardt finished twelfth in the points, while intense young underdog Alan Kulwicki won the title by just ten points over the better-funded Junior Johnson team and driver Bill Elliott.

The win at Charlotte was the forty-sixth for crew chief Kirk Shelmerdine, and it was to be his last with Dale Earnhardt. The pressure on crew chiefs at the top of the Winston Cup Series is nearly unimaginable, and by the end of the 1992 season, Shelmerdine had had enough. In an interview midway through the season, Kirk referred to the demands that eventually led to his decision to resign from Richard Childress Racing.

"We never really get a chance to stand outside and look in and realize the pressure we're under," Shelmerdine said of his work, work that had brought Dale Earnhardt so many of his championships and victories. "I would imagine it is quite a bit different than most people would imagine. There is a lot of responsibility that we put on ourselves. It's not really somebody standing right at your heels all of the time, barking; it's not that kind of obvious pressure. But it's there and we're always... There's always so much going on that's in the back of your head all of time that you don't really have time off for recreation, or time to spend with your family

like you should. Friends kind of go by the wayside because you don't pay enough attention to them. Life is different."

With Shelmerdine gone, Richard Childress knew his team was in disarray and needed immediate help. He turned to Andy Petree. Petree had been crew chief for Leo Jackson's team and had engineered Harry Gant's brilliant September streak in 1991. The combination of Petree and Earnhardt had plenty of potential. But would that potential be realized?

After starting the Petree era with two runner-up finishes, Earnhardt suffered through two disappointing runs. Talk spread that Petree was not able to get Richard Childress Racing back on the winning track, or if he was, it would still be a year or two before the team truly became competitive. After all, even one bad season can set a team back so far that it takes years to fully recover. But at Darlington, some indications of the future were revealed, and not just for Earnhardt.

In what would soon become a common feature in Winston Cup racing, Mark Martin and young driver Jeff Gordon were battling for the victory all day at Darlington. But Martin's tenacity and Gordon's emerging talent were no match for a driver with a tremendous record at this most demanding of speedways. Dale dominated the last

Opposite: Dale Earnhardt pitches in to help set his car up for a race. It's a task that he had been accustomed to ever since he was a small child helping his father—it was part of his racing heritage.

third of the race, ending an eight-month drought without a Winston Cup win. Earnhardt assumed command of the points race, leading Rusty Wallace by fifty-seven points.

But erratic performances began to haunt the team again. Bad runs at North Wilkesboro and Martinsville led up to the race at Talladega, where Earnhardt had had great success before. This time he managed to finish fourth, but the big story was what happened just short of the finish line.

NASCAR had stopped the cars for a brief rain shower. Once the track was dry, the green flag turned the stock cars loose with just two laps remaining. As the cars built speed, the potential for chaos in close quarters was realized. Battling for the lead were Earnhardt, Martin, Wallace, Jimmy Spencer, Dale Jarrett, Joe Ruttman, and more. Contact was made again and again on the final lap, but the most devastating event was yet to come. Earnhardt and Winston Cup points leader Wallace tried to move into the same space at the same time, Dale's front hitting Wallace's rear. At nearly two hundred mph (321.8kph), Wallace's car became airborne, then disintegrated as it performed a sickening series of rolls in front of the tri-oval grandstands. "I was going for the hole, and he cut down," Earnhardt explained. "I hit him in the left rear bumper and it turned him upside-down. It was more my fault than anything, but I didn't do it on purpose. Rusty and I are good friends. I can understand why his crew is mad."

The crew was mad because their points-leading driver had just suffered a broken wrist, a concussion, and myriad cuts and bruises as a result of what they felt was a dangerous move by someone trying to steal back the points lead. Wallace himself, though, was diplomatic. "We had both fallen back," Wallace said, "and we were trying to get back to the front. When I moved over to block Dale, he was going four or five miles per hour [6.44 or 8.04kph] faster than I was. If it was anyone's fault, it was mine."

Regardless of the controversy, Earnhardt had cut his championship deficit to eighty-six points.

A return to victory lane came at Charlotte's six-hundred-mile (965.4km) race, though Dale had to battle past three penalties. NASCAR determined that Earnhardt had indulged in rough driving in an incident with Greg Sacks, and he was hit with a one-lap penalty. Later, Dale was penalized for going too fast on pit road, and the third penalty came when the crew had too many workers over the wall on a pit stop. Despite the obstacles, Earnhardt held off Jeff Gordon for the win.

The team was functioning like the Childress operation had at its peak. Signs that new heights were within reach came when Dale won the next race, at Dover. On July 3, his brilliance at negotiating the tricky aerodynamic currents of super-speedway racing was on display, and the black Lumina won at Daytona. A scant two weeks later, Pocono International Raceway fell victim to the Earnhardt assault. A week later, Earnhardt tasted victory at Talladega.

Down the championship stretch of the season, it became clear that the contenders for the title were Earnhardt and Wallace. At Daytona, Wallace, still recovering from the crash at Talladega, was 273 points behind Earnhardt. But by the beginning of October, when Rusty and Dale finished first and second, respectively, at North Wilkesboro, Wallace had cut the deficit to seventy-two points. The two completed the race at North Carolina Motor Speedway in the same order.

Left: Two of the greatest drivers in the history of the Winston Cup Series, Dale Earnhardt and "The King," Richard Petty. Though Earnhardt tied Petty's mark of seven NASCAR championships, Richard's NASCAR-leading mark of 200 career wins reamins unchallenged.

NASCAR championships. The Richard Childress Racing team and crew chief Andy Petree were poised to make history in 1994.

At Atlanta Motor Speedway in the final race of the year, Wallace took his last best shot at Earnhardt, winning the race; it was his tenth victory of the year. But Earnhardt drove well enough to claim the title by eighty points. His six victories and twenty-one top-ten finishes gave him the margin he needed to claim his sixth championship.

It had been a trying year in the Winston Cup Series. Defending Winston Cup champion Alan Kulwicki died in a plane crash flying to Bristol in April. Rising young superstar Davey Allison died in July, the victim of a helicopter accident. As if to show what really mattered in stock car racing, after the checkered flag fell, both Dale Earnhardt and Rusty Wallace slowly circled the track, each driver waving a flag showing the car numbers of Kulwicki and Allison.

Now Dale Earnhardt had closed to within one title of tying Richard Petty's mark of seven

The first win of the year came at the track that had been so harsh to so many Winston Cup drivers but had always seemed kind to Dale Earnhardt. "Too Tough to Tame," "The Lady in Black"— Darlington Raceway is known by many names.

"You can call this old racetrack a lot of nick-names, and she deserves them," Earnhardt said after winning at the historic track for the ninth time.

"If you respect her and run consistent, you'll have a chance of winning. David Pearson taught me that—to use my head every lap and race the track and not the other competitors."

The victory was bittersweet. Earnhardt dedicated his win to the memory of one of his best friends, Neil Bonnett. The great Winston Cup driver had been killed at Daytona the month before.

As the 1994 Winston Cup season picked up speed, a script similar to 1993's was being written, as Dale won the next race on the schedule at Bristol.

The victory, which saw Ken Schrader come in a distant second, gave Earnhardt the points lead for what he hoped would be a seventh championship. Another win in yet another wild race at Talladega edged him even closer.

"There was so much passing going on the last lap I didn't know who was passing who," Dale said after narrowly beating Ernie Irvan to the checkered flag. "Luckily we wound up in front. It's especially exciting to win such a competitive race."

Dale Earnhardt had won championships in the past by pounding out win after win, but he also knew that consistency was equally important. With Petree and Childress overseeing the preparation of Earnhardt's Luminas, the team did not appear in the winner's circle for months in the wake of Talladega. But where they did appear was in the top of the finishing order, week after week after week. The slow and steady accumulation of points gave Earnhardt an opportunity to lock up the championship at North Carolina Motor Speedway in October. Dale wanted to do it in style.

Starting deep in the field in twentieth place, Earnhardt worked hard all afternoon, moving forward with steady determination. At the end it came down to a dogged battle with Rick Mast, anxious to win his first Winston Cup race. But when Earnhardt senses an opportunity for victory, he is almost unstoppable. Dale Earnhardt won the race and clinched a record-tying seventh Winston Cup championship.

"Now we can talk about it all day," a happily relieved Earnhardt said of the mark, which he had been reluctant to discuss. But even though the pressure was off, Dale didn't have an easy explanation of what the feat really meant to him.

"You can't sum it up in just a word or phrase," Earnhardt noted. "It's going to take a long time to sink in."

Clearly, Dale Earnhardt was on top of the NASCAR world. But the fact that he had just won his seventh championship was undeniable proof that he was one of the sport's most experienced veterans, and there is always young blood anxious to write their own legends at the expense of the veterans.

When Alan Kulwicki won the 1992 championship at Atlanta Motor Speedway, it was Richard

Below: Teresa Earnhardt was an ideal partner for Dale. Her family's racing background allowed her to understand her husband's career from the beginning, and her intelligence and poise helped ensure Dale's success both on and off the track.

Petty's final race. Most of the media attention had quite naturally focused on those big stories, but deep in the starting field that November day, a young driver had made his first start in a bright, multicolored Chevrolet. That driver was Jeff Gordon.

During the 1993 season, Gordon had shown flashes of brilliance that pointed to a bright future in the Winston Cup Series. By 1994, while Earnhardt was chasing down Petty's record of seven titles, Gordon had graduated from contender to winner. His first victory came with an emotional win in the six-hundred-mile (965.4km) race at Charlotte Motor Speedway, based on the crafty pit strategy of his brilliant crew chief, Ray Evernham. Gordon's

Below: Dale Earnhardt and Terry Labonte compare notes in 1997. A less amicable conversation took place between the two in 1999 after Earnhardt made contact with Labonte on the last lap at Bristol Motor Speedway, stealing what looked to be an almost certain victory from Labonte.

team backed up that first win by claiming the first Brickyard 400 after outdueling Ernie Irvan at the famed Indianapolis Motor Speedway later in the season. Gordon's high-profile win in his adopted home state was tremendously popular, but more important, it signaled that the young driver was ready to contend for a championship. And while Earnhardt had his sights set on an eighth title, Gordon was determined to win his first in 1995.

Earnhardt had a characteristically strong season, as his fans had come to expect. He ran at the front of the pack in each race, and he finally clawed his way to victory lane with a hard-fought race at North Wilkesboro. The problem was, Jeff Gordon had already won three races.

"We've finally won one," Dale said after the Wilkesboro win. "It's amazing, we finally beat 'Wonder Boy.' "

Wonder Boy became the nickname by which Gordon was referred to by Dale's fans and many others who weren't especially pleased to see the well-funded upstart beating their heroes week after week. But Gordon didn't seem too concerned with what the fans or Dale Earnhardt were calling him; he displayed a focused maturity rare in a young driver. And he had the Winston Cup championship points lead.

Dale did what he could to derail the Gordon Express, even managing to win for the first time at a road course when he passed Mark Martin late in the race at Sears Point, California.

Jeff Gordon wanted to repeat his triumph of the year before when the Winston Cup Series returned to Indianapolis Motor Speedway. But Earnhardt thwarted him and the rest of the drivers, winning the second Brickyard 400.

"To win this race is great," an excited Earnhardt exclaimed. "This Richard Childress Racing team is hard to beat when we're right."

A master of psychological intimidation, Earnhardt made a pointed jab at young Gordon's win in the inaugural Brickyard 400, joking that his victory made him the first man to win the Indianapolis race.

But Gordon refused to crumble under the pressure. Though Dale won again in September at Martinsville, Gordon left the Virginia track with a 275-point lead and just five races left in the season.

It came down to the final race of the year, as it has so often before. And again in familiar fashion,

Below: Jeff Gordon, Terry Labonte's Hendrick Motorsports teammate, battled Dale for the championship in 1995. Gordon (left) won the title, despite Earnhardt's best attempts to rattle the young driver.

Dale Earnhardt was the strongest driver, easily winning at Atlanta Motor Speedway. But it wasn't enough. Jeff Gordon had driven his Hendrick Motorsports Chevrolet with poise and determination all year. Even though he faltered in the last race, finishing thirty-second, Jeff Gordon had amassed enough points to win his first Winston Cup Series championship, by thirty-four points over Earnhardt.

"It's good to end a season so clean," Dale stated in the aftermath of the Atlanta race, "but don't ask what it's like finishing second in points. Everybody knows what I think of second."

Though delivered in a good-natured way, Earnhardt couldn't resist firing one last shot at the young driver who had kept him from winning his eighth title: "Gordon is so young they're going to serve his team milk at the banquet in New York instead of champagne."

Prior to the 1996 season, Andy Petree, the man who had guided the team so capably in the wake of

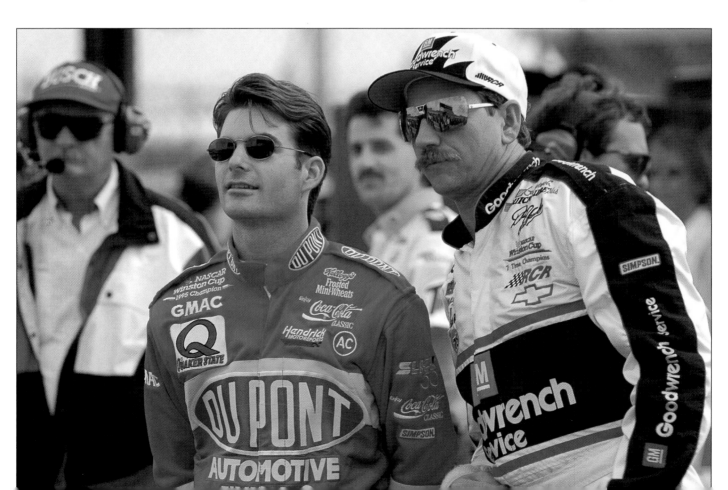

crew chief Kirk Shelmerdine's departure, also left Richard Childress Racing. Petree had climbed into high regard when he masterminded Harry Gant's 1991 winning streak with the Leo Jackson team. Now Jackson had offered Petree the opportunity to assume ownership of the team. It was an offer Petree could not turn down.

Though a crew chief's departure can be upsetting, it didn't seem to disrupt the winning ways of the Childress team. Dale won at both Rockingham and Atlanta early in the 1996 season. But at the most fearsome of all NASCAR tracks, disaster struck.

It was July 26. Dale was furiously fighting for the lead at Talladega Superspeedway, the fastest of all NASCAR tracks. Contact with Sterling Marlin sent Dale's black Monte Carlo almost head-on into the wall at two hundred mph (321.8kph). The car

flipped, sliding and ricocheting like a pinball among the other cars in a horrendous crash. The Childress machine eventually wound up back on all four wheels, but the mangled mass of metal was testament to the violence of the crash.

Miraculously, Earnhardt emerged with assistance from the wreckage and made it to the ambulance under his own power. But he was severely injured, the bruises and lacerations made worse by a broken collarbone and sternum.

"When I turned abruptly into the wall is when I broke my sternum," Earnhardt recalled days later at Indianapolis Motor Speedway. "Then the car got up on its side and slid along and I could see the asphalt pavement through the window net.

"I hunkered down as much as I could and I was gripping the steering wheel with both hands to keep

from being thrown around in the cockpit, because I knew the following cars were going to hit me."

Most drivers would not have been able to even consider racing in the wake of such a devastating crash, but Dale Earnhardt started the Brickyard 400 less than a week later. He had to yield the driver's seat for relief in what he calls one of the most distressing moments of his career, allowing Mike Skinner to take the wheel of the black Chevrolet.

"It's hard to get out of that car," an emotional Earnhardt told a national television audience moments after painfully climbing from the stock car. "This is my life, right here."

Though Dale was disappointed that he had to turn over his car to another driver, the fact that he had even started the race was astonishing. And a week later, he qualified on the pole at the demand-

ing Watkins Glen road course. Earnhardt not only started this event, he drove the entire race to come home in sixth place. It was one of the most courageous performances in stock car racing history.

Dale Earnhardt did not win again in 1996, and many pointed to the severity of his injuries in the horrible crash at Talladega as the cause. But he did not win in 1997 either. Whispers began to circulate that Earnhardt had lost his edge. A bizarre incident at Darlington Raceway late in the season (Dale became disoriented, hit the wall, and then had difficulty getting the car back to pit road) only increased the rumblings.

At season's end, Earnhardt had no wins and sixteen top-ten finishes. Any other driver might have been happy with the top-tens, but not Dale.

To be sure, it had been a frustrating season. Earnhardt desperately wanted to get back to victory lane. But his first chance would come in an event he had found impossible to win: the first race of the season, the Daytona 500. For Earnhardt, the Daytona 500 had become the very definition of frustration.

Above: A personal message from Stevie Waltrip, wife of past champion Darrell Waltrip, awaited Earnhardt's entrance to his workplace on this day.

Opposite: Though Dale was one of the greatest stock car drivers of all times, he was not adverse to a little hard work, as this photograph of the seven-time Winston Cup champion shows.

MAN VERSUS RACETRACK

Most stock car drivers would agree that each racetrack has its own personality. Some tracks are forgiving, allowing drivers to easily race three abreast. Others are less kind.

Almost every driver in the Winston Cup Series can attest to the cruelty of The Lady in Black, Darlington Raceway. The Darlington Stripe—a scrape along the outside of a stock car's body, received when the car brushes the outside wall—is a badge unwillingly adopted by almost all who have challenged the legendary South Carolina speedway.

But all the legends of great drivers battling the quirks of high-banked pavement pale when compared to Dale Earnhardt's quest to master the greatest prize at stock car racing's most famous superspeedway, Daytona International.

The Daytona 500 is NASCAR's most prestigious race, and the list of those who have visited victory lane reads like a *Who's Who* of the sport. Dale Earnhardt's determination to add his own name to that list made for one of the most exciting, and most frustrating and heartbreaking, tales of stock car racing.

Earnhardt first took on The Great American Race in 1979. Young Dale was at the wheel of Rod Osterlund's Buick, and the number 2 stock car found itself in the midst of elite NASCAR company. Among those Earnhardt squared off against were masters of the sport of stock car racing: Richard Petty, Bobby and Donnie Allison, A.J. Foyt, Buddy Baker, Cale Yarborough, David Pearson, and Benny Parsons.

If the man soon to be known as The Intimidator was himself intimidated by such fast company, he didn't show it. Although the national focus was on Petty's victory and the brouhaha in the infield as the Allisons scrapped with Yarborough after a late-race crash, Dale Earnhardt brought his Buick home with a highly respectable eighth-place finish, just one lap off the pace. It was an improvement from his tenth-place starting position, and an impressive performance for a driver starting in just his tenth NASCAR Winston Cup Series event.

Though Daytona International Speedway had seemed to take a liking to Dale Earnhardt running in her greatest event, this would be just the first step in a long and torturous journey that evolved into a determined quest for victory.

In 1980, Buddy Baker set a Daytona 500 race record as he cruised to a win at more than 177 mph (284.79kph). But Earnhardt was in the mix, charging from a disappointing thirty-second starting position to lead on seven separate occasions. Dale started the charge to his first championship by finishing fourth in the 500, an improvement over the year before.

Pages 74–75: Richard Childress built on his success with Dale Earnhardt by adding a second Winston Cup team, this one featuring driver Mike Skinner. Here the two Childress cars lead the field at Martinsville Speedway.

Opposite: Though he had won nearly every imaginable race held at Daytona International Speedway, victory in the Daytona 500 slipped through Earnhardt's determined fingers year after year.

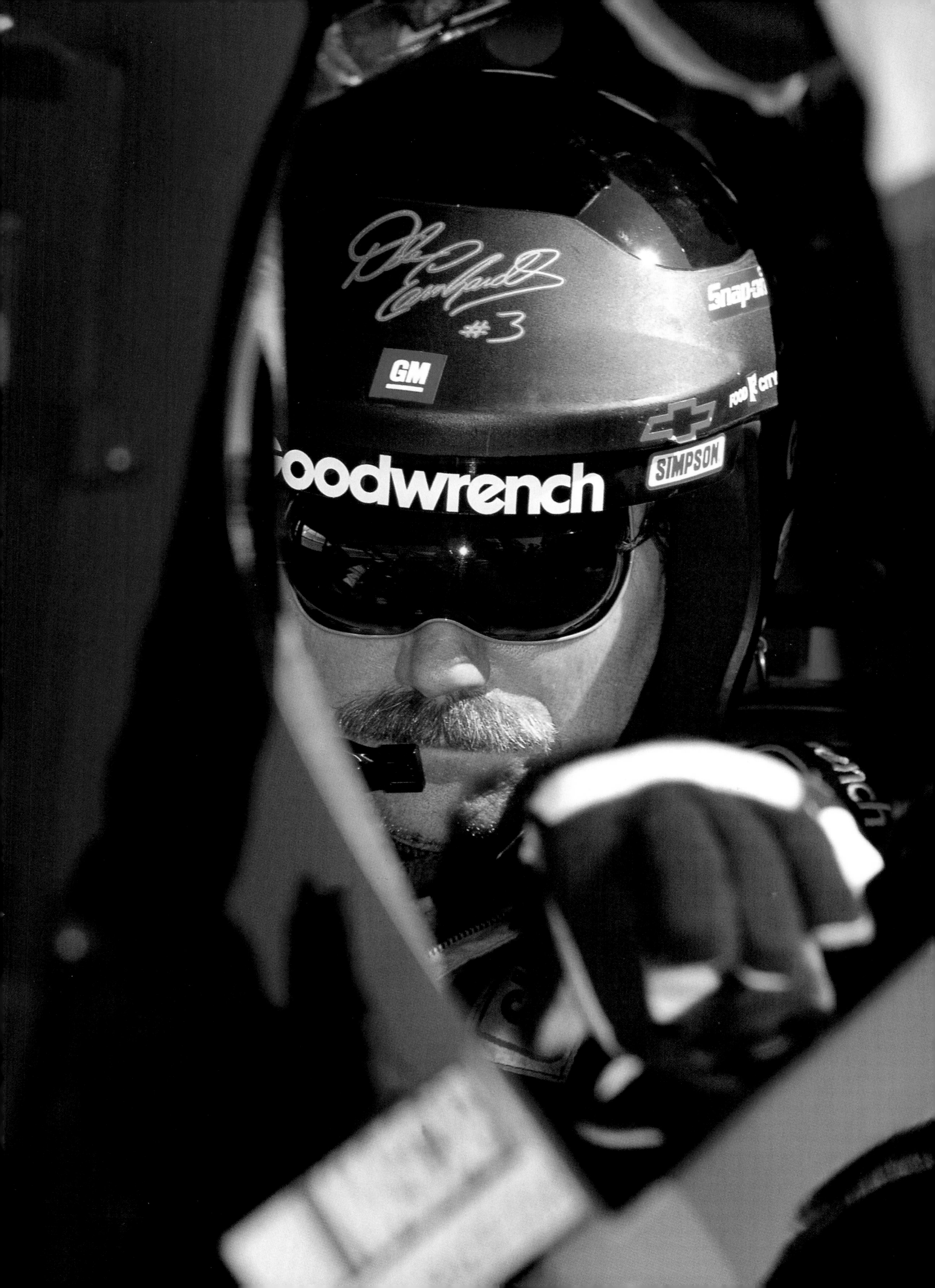
GM
#3
oodwrench
SIMPSON

Fresh from winning the 1980 championship, Earnhardt took on the 1981 Daytona 500 in bright new Wrangler colors and one of the new downsized Pontiacs. Dale again led the race and was a contender, but Richard Petty and crew chief Dale Inman out-foxed the field. When all of the leaders, including Earnhardt, pitted for gas and tires on the final pit stop, Inman made the call for Petty to stop just long enough to take on the fuel needed to complete the twenty laps remaining in the race, gambling that the STP car's tires would last. They did, and Earnhardt had to settle for fifth place, crossing the line just behind Bobby Allison, Ricky Rudd, and Buddy Baker.

If Dale had grown accustomed to Daytona 500 top-ten finishes, a rude awakening came in 1982, when he was driving for Bud Moore. The Ford powerplant under the hood expired after Earnhardt had completed just forty-four of two hundred laps, leaving him with a disappointing thirty-sixth-place finish as Bobby Allison drove to the win. The same fate befell the team a year later, after sixty-three laps. Dale's finish in the 1983 Daytona 500 standings improved by a single position, which was little consolation. Cale Yarborough was more fortunate, taking millions of TV viewers with him to victory, thanks to an early version of the in-car television camera.

Cale repeated in 1984, but this time he had more company than just TV viewers. Closing in on his rear bumper was Dale Earnhardt, in his new Richard

Right: In a characteristically determined pose, Dale peers out from the cockpit in 1991, yet another frustrating year in the Intimidator's quest for a Daytona 500 victory.

Childress Chevrolet. Though the charge fell short, it was Earnhardt's best Daytona 500 finish in years.

But the good run of 1984 was just a memory in 1985, when the Richard Childress Racing engine failed after eighty-four laps, leaving Dale in thirty-second place as Bill Elliott drive on to win his first Daytona 500.

It looked like Dale might finally get his first win in the Daytona 500 in 1986. Though caution flags slowed the first half of the event, a long period of green-flag racing set two drivers apart from the pack. Dale Earnhardt and Geoff Bodine looked to be the class of the field, and a shootout appeared imminent as the laps wound down. Earnhardt pestered Bodine and was doing a good job of making the New York driver worry about when Dale would make his move. But Dale never got the chance. With just three laps left in the race, his Childress stock car ran out of fuel. And in a final insult, once the car had been fueled, Dale's motor broke as he left pit road. Earnhardt went home credited with thirteenth place; Bodine went to victory lane.

"I knew Dale had a strong car," Geoff admitted. "He was trying all kinds of tricks behind me to make my car loose, and he was doing a good job of it. When he ran out of gas, I was relieved."

"I think we could have beaten him, but we stretched our gas supply a little too much," Dale noted. Still, the strong run set the pace for the season, as Earnhardt drove on to the series championship.

In 1987, it was Bodine whose fuel ran out with three laps remaining. He surrendered the lead to Bill Elliott, who won the Daytona 500 again. Earnhardt

watched the events unfold from fifth place, close but not close enough. Though Dale won eleven times on his way to another Winston Cup championship that season, once again the Daytona 500 was not one of his victories.

Another decent finish awaited the Goodwrench Chevrolet in 1988—a decent finish, but still not a win after ten years of trying. As Bobby Allison drove to victory and Richard Petty survived a horrifying accident, Dale settled for tenth place.

Four Chevys swept the top positions in 1989, but the car in first belonged to Darrell Waltrip. Conserving fuel, Waltrip made it more than 130 miles to the checkered flag. He inherited the lead when the faster cars of Ken Schrader and Dale Earnhardt were forced to pit for fuel with just ten laps left. Schrader was runner-up to Waltrip, with Earnhardt close behind. Again, Dale had come so close, and again he was frustrated by the vagaries of stock car racing.

Yet if Earnhardt had found his first eleven attempts to be frustrating, a much more heartbreaking finish was waiting for him the very next year.

The 1990 Daytona 500 truly looked to belong to Dale Earnhardt. His car was very fast, the Kirk Shelmerdine-led pit crew was speedy and sure, and Earnhardt was on top of his game. Dale had built up a lead of more than twenty seconds late in event. Even a late-race caution was of no concern, as Earnhardt closed in on the win.

Derrick Cope was behind Earnhardt, trying to hold off Terry Labonte and Bill Elliott for second place. Cope was sure Earnhardt had the race wrapped

up. The cars took the white flag, beginning the final lap. Earnhardt charged on through turns one and two and down the long back straightaway. Victory was his—and then Cope saw something he could hardly believe was actually happening: nearing the final two turns, with just one mile left in the Daytona 500, Derrick Cope saw a rear tire on Earnhardt's black Lumina begin to fail.

"I actually saw everything start to unfold, because I could see the tire start elongating," Cope recalled. "It looked like a drag racing tire, almost. The thing started to elongate and I could tell that the rubber was coming off the rear tire and when I

saw that, at that point, the best thing that I could do was aim for him. Stay with him.

"He kept the car straight," Cope continues. "I was seeing myself inch back up on him and I saw the tire start to elongate and the pieces came back and hit my car, something went through my grille. I could see something come back and hit my car and then I was going to the bottom of the racetrack. I had been going in and the car was going up high and I knew that I had saved the car enough that I felt like I could go to the bottom of the racetrack and stay down there hoping that Labonte and Elliot would go with me. As we went down through there we both started to go to the bottom of the racetrack and I think Earnhardt was trying to give himself a lot of room with the tire going down. We both went to the bottom of the racetrack. I just followed him

Above: At the IROC, racing's greatest drivers compete in identically prepared vehicles. Here, Dale Earnhardt charges down the straightaway at Daytona, passing Alex Zanardi on the outside.

down and his car turned sideways and he turned to the right to get the car up and I stayed to the bottom. I went right to the apron and as I went by him I just hoped he didn't hit me. I didn't know what was going to happen. I went by him and then my car stayed pretty good at the bottom. I looked back to see where Labonte and Elliot were. I figured there was just absolutely no way they could beat me if I kept my foot down all the way to the floor."

Derrick Cope was right; they weren't able to catch him. A relatively unknown driver who had never won a NASCAR Winston Cup race had just won the series' biggest event. And again, Dale Earnhardt had lost.

"We were so close," Dale said. "He won the race but I outran everybody all day. He lucked into it."

"What a heartbreaker," Richard Childress lamented. "To be a half-mile from something you've dreamed about all your life… man, that's awfully hard to take. But that's racing. It'll bite you when you least expect it."

And so the list of Daytona 500 disappointments grew longer. And longer.

In 1991, during a race made confusing by new pit road rules, Ernie Irvan won when Dale spun after making contact with Davey Allison at the front of the field with just two laps left.

Earnhardt's Lumina was heavily damaged in a major crash halfway through the 1992 Daytona 500. Dale still managed to drive the mangled machine to a ninth-place finish, an accomplishment in itself.

The frustration reached a new peak in 1993. After driving well the entire race and giving himself a real shot at winning, Earnhardt's car became slightly loose. Dale Jarrett took advantage of the situation, diving under Earnhardt as the cars began the last lap. When they came around for the checkered flag, Jarrett was able to hold off Earnhardt.

"Big damn deal, I lost another Daytona 500," Earnhardt fumed. "We've lost this race about every way you can lose it. We've been out-gassed, out-tired, out-run, and out-everythinged. We've come close. There's nothing left to do but come back and try again next year."

And try he did in 1994. Late in the race the car was handling even worse than it had the year before. The result was seventh place.

"What can you say?" the great driver reflected. "I just didn't have the car to win it today."

He had the car to win it in 1995—almost. When a late-race caution flag fell, Dale, Childress, and the crew determined his only real chance was to pit for four fresh tires. When the green flag waved again with just ten laps left, things soured and Dale's Chevy finished in fourteenth place.

Then began one of the great charges in Winston Cup Series history. Earnhardt roared up through the pack, passing frontrunner after frontrunner. With

Above: When the familiar black number 3 Monte Carlo was unloaded at Daytona International Speedway in February 1998, many suspected that this year's Richard Childress Racing stock car might give Earnhardt his best chance at winning the Daytona 500.

just over three laps left, he passed Mark Martin and took over second. Dale's sights were set on leader Sterling Marlin, but he ran out of time. For the third time, Dale Earnhardt finished the Daytona 500 in second place.

"This is the Daytona 500, and I don't reckon I'm supposed to win the damn thing," a resigned Earnhardt commented. "If we'd had some drafting help, we might have got by Sterling, but he was awfully strong. I reckon the best car won."

A replay of 1993 came about in 1996. On the last lap, once again it was Earnhardt doing anything he could do to get into the lead, and once again Dale Jarrett was thwarting his moves. Jarrett won his second Daytona 500; Dale placed second for the fourth time.

"I was doing all I could, but every move I made, he moved over to block," Earnhardt explained.

Not that the other drivers were taking it for granted that the Earnhardt Daytona 500 jinx would last forever. Dale Jarrett summed up the respect all the competitors had for Earnhardt.

"The last lap seemed like it was 500 miles," Jarrett acknowledged. "I'd rather see anything than that black number 3 in my mirror."

In 1997, the string of runner-up finishes came to an abrupt end when Earnhardt and Jeff Gordon made contact late in the race. Dale had been in second, but the contact with Gordon's car sent Earnhardt tumbling at two hundred mph (321.8kph). When his car finally came to a rest, Dale emerged and was taken to a waiting ambulance. Then came a moment that defines Earnhardt's competitive spirit and determination.

Noticing that his battered, black stock car was still on all four wheels, Earnhardt walked back over to his racer. One of the track workers was in the driver's seat to help get the car towed back to the garage. Earnhardt leaned over, asked him to try to start the engine. It fired up.

"I said, 'Get out. I gotta go,' " Dale recalled.

After flipping violently at tremendous speed, the battered driver and his even more battered car drove off toward pit road, dignity intact, to the amazement of millions of racing fans and the admiration of his fellow competitors. Though Gordon won the race, Dale triumphed just the same.

The trek to Daytona each February was made more painful for Dale by the question he heard over and over: "When are you going to win the Daytona 500?" As if it were simply a matter of looking into a crystal ball or checking a computer forecast.

And it certainly wasn't a case of Dale Earnhardt being jinxed at Daytona International Speedway. Other than the Daytona 500 itself, Dale had won just about every race held at the imposing, 2.5-mile (4.02km) superspeedway. Earnhardt had visited Daytona's victory lane after winning the Firecracker 400 in July, the Twin 125 qualifying races leading up to the Daytona 500, the International Race of Champions all-star race, and the three-hundred-mile (482.7km) Busch Series race held the day before the 500. Still, it began to seem quite conceivable that Dale might never win the Daytona 500.

When Dale Earnhardt arrived in Daytona for the 1998 Daytona 500, he faced the same barrage of questions. Would this be the year?

Earnhardt seemed characteristically calm as the big day neared. And just as characteristic, on the Thursday before the Daytona 500, he won one of the 125-mile (201.12km) qualifying races for the ninth straight year. Though he'd pulled off that win many times before only to encounter failure in the 500, after his 1998 victory in the shorter race Dale was confident about his chances.

"We're going to start our winning streak here at Daytona and go on from that," Earnhardt vowed. "I'm ready to start."

He was indeed ready to start. From the moment the green flag waved, millions of race fans watched as Earnhardt demonstrated he was a top contender to win the Daytona 500. But that was nothing new; he had proven that every year. Everyone knew all that mattered was where the black Monte Carlo would be when the checkered flag fell two hundred laps later.

Past the halfway point of the race, Earnhardt powered into the lead again on lap 140, driving past Mike Skinner. There he sat, out front in the Daytona 500, a position he had held so many times before only to see some unimaginable incident unfold and deny him his win.

When a caution flag waved with just over twenty laps remaining, Earnhardt was into the pits and back out in first. The green flag waved again on lap 178. Every driver behind him knew that catching Dale Earnhardt was one thing; passing him was another entirely. But that didn't mean they weren't going to try.

Above: Time to reflect before the Daytona 500 is a rarity, especially for Dale Earnhardt, who for years was surrounded by members of the media asking him the same question again and again: "Can you win the Daytona 500?"

It was quite possibly one of the greatest battles in stock car racing history, Dale Earnhardt against all of the other top drivers of the Winston Cup Series. Again and again he fended off challenges, battling the turbulent aerodynamics of two hundred-mph (321.8kph) racing as driver after driver drafted forward to try to steal away the lead. Through it all, Dale clung to his chance of winning, blocking passes, putting his car where it needed to be to maintain its greatest momentum.

Suddenly, contact between Jimmy Spencer and John Andretti sent Andretti and Lake Speed into spins. The caution lights came on, and the front

Above: With Rusty Wallace and Jeremy Mayfield riding his rear bumper, Dale Earnhardt drafts past Jeff Gordon as the laps pile up in the 1998 Daytona 500. A furious charge to the checkered flag was in the works.

pack was now racing back toward both the yellow flag and the white flag, which indicated that just a single lap remained in the race. Whoever reached the finish line first would almost certainly win the Daytona 500.

With a renewed frenzy, the shuffling on Earnhardt's back bumper went on. As the cars closed on the finish, Bobby Labonte's Pontiac managed to get by Jeremy Mayfield's Ford. Labonte had mounted a strong charge, but he was too late. Dale Earnhardt flashed across the line first.

The cars had taken both the yellow and white flags when they came across the line. The race would end under caution, but Dale still had to follow the pace car around the 2.5-mile (4.02km) track and back to the finish line. It seemed unlikely that anything could go wrong now—but hadn't so many of the improbable things that had prevented Dale from winning the Daytona 500 in the past seemed just as unlikely? Everyone held their breath as the black number 3 car slowly negotiated a final lap around Daytona International Speedway.

"I knew we were coming back to the checkered," Dale recalled after the race. "I started going slow, but then I decided I would go fast because I wanted to get on back around there."

He did, and twenty years of disappointment came to an end when Dale's Monte Carlo crossed the finish line. It was one of the most popular wins in NASCAR history, and not just among the race fans. When Earnhardt reached pit row, hundreds of crew members from the other race teams lined the pits and extended their hands to congratulate the great driver.

"I cried a little bit in the race car on the way to the checkered flag," Dale said. "Well, maybe not cried, but at least my eyes watered up."

Though he had been crowned Winston Cup Series champion seven times, though he had won dozens of poles and dozens of races, though he had mastered the toughest racetracks of the Winston Cup Series, there had been one achievement missing from Earnhardt's racing records. On February 15, 1998, that was no longer the case.

Dale Earnhardt was the winner of the 1998 Daytona 500.

Below: At last, triumph! From atop his Daytona 500-winning Monte Carlo, Dale Earnhardt jubilantly surveys victory lane.

A WINNING LEGACY

Though all of Dale Earnhardt's children (save youngest daughter Taylor Nicole) have tried their hand at racing, son Dale Earnhardt Jr. has shown the requisite talent and determination to carve his own niche in NASCAR. But the Winston Cup Series that Dale Jr. now competes in has changed so much since it was founded fifty years ago that it is nearly unrecognizable as the same sport. His father, while winning seven championships, witnessed much of stock car racing's evolution into a corporate sport. What he saw doubtlessly helped Dale Jr. avoid many of the pitfalls on what can be a treacherous proving ground.

Of course, Dale Earnhardt's advice was never limited to family members. Many drivers of the Winston Cup Series recall the help they received from Earnhardt over the years.

Whether helping along the careers of his children or his colleagues, Earnhardt was always looking to the future. Not surprisingly, he built a racing team that quickly became one of Winston Cup racing's more successful outfits.

Entering competition in 1997, Earnhardt's Winston Cup team was founded with driver Steve

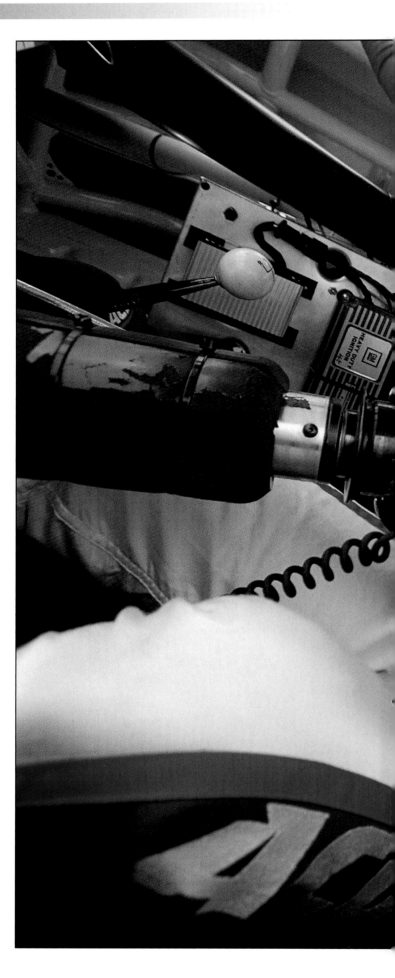

Right: More than mere family resemblance, the posture and equipment of Dale Earnhardt Jr. all call to mind the historic feats of his father. Many race fans are certain that Dale Earnhardt Jr. will carry on the family tradition of winning.

Park, a young New York driver chosen by Dale for the potential he had shown in strong runs in NASCAR's Modified, Truck, and Busch series competition. When Dale tried to reach Park to offer him this extremely desirable position, Park refused to call the great Earnhardt back. Was he intimidated by the thought of driving for Dale? No, he just couldn't believe that Earnhardt was offering him this coveted ride and assumed it was a friend playing a prank.

Dale Earnhardt built a state-of-the-art facility for his new Winston Cup team. Located near Mooresville, North Carolina, Dale Earnhardt Incorporated opened with a racing operation sprawled over 500,000 square feet (46,451.5m²), employing more than 150 people. It was a far cry from the days when Ralph Earnhardt would load his race car from his small garage onto a trailer, tow it to the track, race it, then tow it home so young Dale could help clean it.

Though Park, like any young driver, had his ups and downs establishing his Winston Cup career, he began to place solidly during Winston Cup races in 1998 and 1999. And the Dale Earnhardt Incorporated forces gained strength for the year 2000 with the addition of another young driver who was already a two-time Busch Grand National champion. His name was Dale Earnhardt Jr.

Dale Jr. had made his debut in a Winston Cup car late in 1998, racing about as far from North Carolina as you can get. Competing in an exhibition race in Motegi, Japan, Earnhardt competed

Above: Dale Jr. paved the way for his full-time entrance into the Winston Cup Series in 2000 by claiming his second consecutive Busch Grand National title in 1999, once again battling Matt Kenseth to the crown.

head-to-head against his father for the first time. Dale Jr. finished sixth at Motegi, and later scored his first Winston Cup top-ten at Richmond during one of a handful of Winston Cup starts in 1999.

Driving his red Chevrolet in 2000, Dale Jr. soon served notice that the immense talent of his father had been passed on. In just the seventh race of the season, Dale Jr. raced to victory at Texas Motor Speedway. Four races later, he proved the win was no fluke with a second victory, this time in Richmond, Virginia. In addition to the two victories, Dale Jr. scored three top-tens in his debut season.

Park was also up to the challenge, and eager to match Dale Jr.'s accomplishments. On August 13 at Watkins Glen, Steve Park's yellow Monte Carlo streaked across the finish line to bring Dale Earnhardt Incorporated its third win of the 2000 season. Park proceeded to tally eleven top-tens that season.

Despite the success, though, the real passion of Dale Earnhardt's life was to sit behind the wheel of a Winston Cup Series stock car. With his long-term driving contract with Richard Childress, Earnhardt looked to continue the alliance that had already lasted two decades well into the new millennium.

Though Dale Sr. built on his success in 1998 with three wins in 1999, his championship points quest put him at seventh place in the standings, too far behind eventual champion Dale Jarrett for Earnhardt's liking. For the year 2000, Earnhardt knew consistency would be the key to making an eighth title a reality.

Above: No matter how quickly Dale Jr. adapts to Winston Cup competition, he has a long road to travel if he ever hopes to leave behind a legacy to rival that of his father, one of the greatest NASCAR drivers of all time.

A disappointing run in the Daytona 500 did not discourage Earnhardt, and he followed the season opener with a second-place finish at Rockingham, North Carolina. Two weeks later, he was in victory lane for the first time in the 2000 season, holding off a hard-charging Bobby Labonte in a dramatic photo finish at Atlanta Motor Speedway.

Labonte, though, had his own hopes for a Winston Cup championship. Driving a car owned by former National Football League coach Joe

Gibbs, Labonte put together a season that defined consistency—and luck—in the year 2000.

Dale Earnhardt never gave up. His black Chevrolet dogged Labonte all season, but five finishes of twentieth or worse made the title chase an exercise in futility. Earnhardt finished second in the series, just 265 points behind his rival.

Still, Earnhardt had impressed everyone with the title chase. And his legend had grown with his performance on October 15 in the Winston 500 at Alabama's Talladega Superspeedway.

With just fifteen laps remaining in the race, the cars took the green flag after a caution period at the massive superspeedway, NASCAR's fastest track. Earnhardt found himself deep in the field. As the cars hurtled toward race's end, Dale was still mired in eighteenth place with just five laps remaining. He then mounted one of the most astounding stock car charges ever witnessed, powering his way past car after car in a furious surge toward the front. When the checkered flag waved, it flew over the black number 3 Monte Carlo. This time, even Dale himself seemed taken aback by his accomplishment.

"I was very lucky," Earnhardt admitted. "To think we could be eighteenth five laps from the end and win like that is beyond me."

Dale was unquestionably proud of the 2000 performances of Park and his son, but he decided to take another step forward for the 2001 season by adding Michael Waltrip to the Dale Earnhardt team. But some eyebrows were raised by Earnhardt's selection—in a Winston Cup career that had begun in 1985, Waltrip was winless in 462 points races. And Dale had passed over Ron Hornaday, the Truck Series champion who had driven Earnhardt's Busch Series car to several 2000 wins. Clearly, Earnhardt saw something in Waltrip. Equally clearly, Waltrip was under considerable pressure to deliver results for his new boss.

The 2001 Winston Cup season began under clear blue Florida skies on February 18, as the green flag waved to begin the Daytona 500. Dale Earnhardt, determined to capture an elusive eighth championship, was at the front of the field all day in his Richard Childress Racing Chevrolet. Joining him near the front were his drivers, Dale Jr. and Michael Waltrip. Steve Park, in the third Earnhardt car, looked to be a threat himself until he was caught up in a massive late-race crash.

The laps began to wind down until just five remained. At the front, Michael Waltrip clung to the lead, determined by the thought that his first victory might come in NASCAR's greatest race. Dale Jr. ran close behind in second, Dale Sr. in third.

As the field took the white flag for the final lap, the order remained the same. But breathing down the elder Earnhardt's neck was a pack of determined drivers led by Sterling Marlin, Rusty Wallace, and Ken Schrader. Some have since speculated that Earnhardt made a conscious decision to hold off the drivers behind him, giving his son and Waltrip the opportunity to settle it between themselves.

Waltrip and Dale Jr. thundered on toward the start/finish line, while the black Goodwrench car was surrounded by Marlin on the low side, with Wallace and Schrader above. Heading into the last turn, Dale Earnhardt's car slowly veered left. He struggled to control the car in the seconds that followed, but the Monte Carlo moved to the right and began a sudden, horrifying climb toward Schrader's car and the wall beyond.

In victory lane moments later, Michael Waltrip celebrated, anxious to share his victory with the greatest stock car driver of all, the man who had believed in his talents and given him the car that had won the Daytona 500. He had no way of knowing that the worst had happened. Dale Earnhardt had died from injuries suffered in the horrific collision with the wall.

Below: *Before the 2001 Daytona 500, Dale Earnhardt was confident and relaxed as the sport he helped build was about to begin its first full season with one of the big television networks.*

In the hours that followed, the reality of Dale Earnhardt's passing sank in. Race fans were now left only with cherished memories of his great career. Many pointed to a favorite moment, the 1999 International Race of Champions event in Michigan.

In that race, Dale Earnhardt had battled a fellow driver right to the finish line in a heated chase that featured wheel-to-wheel combat and several instances of contact. The other driver? The 1998 NASCAR Busch Grand National Series champion, Dale Earnhardt Jr.

"The last several laps he was on me," Dale said of his son's charge in an interview with ESPN's Dr. Jerry Punch. "I knew he was trying to do something, and the guys were on him. I was protecting the low line going into turn three, and he drove to the outside. All it was was a drag race back to the start/finish line. We sort of scrubbed some fenders and raced back, and it was fun."

The victory had been important, as had been the fun of competing against his own son. But perhaps remembering his own youth and the precious few times he had had the pleasure of racing against his father, Ralph, Dale Earnhardt put the thrilling finish into a personal perspective. "You make memories like that, things you can talk about for all your life."

The evening of his father's passing, a shaken Dale Earnhardt Jr. spoke to the nation of his family's pain. "I appreciate everybody's thoughts and prayers, and we'll get through this," he said. Then Dale Jr. spoke of his father, the man who had defined modern stock car racing. "I'm sure he'd want us to keep going, so that's what we're going to do."

Below: Dale Earnhardt (riding on the inside of Ken Schrader's number 36 M&M's car) was poised for another brilliant finish in the Daytona 500 as this shot from the last lap of that race shows. Then tragedy struck, and within seconds the greatest active driver in the sport was dead, the victim of a high-speed collision with the retaining wall.

Dale Earnhardt's Career Stats (through 1999)

YEARLY WINS AND POINTS TOTALS

Year	Races	Wins	Top 5's	Top 10's	Points Pos.
1979	27	1	11	17	7
1980	31	5	19	24	1
1981	31	0	9	17	7
1982	30	1	7	12	12
1983	30	2	9	14	8
1984	30	2	12	2	4
1985	28	4	1	16	8
1986	29	5	16	23	1
1987	29	11	21	24	1
1988	29	3	13	19	3
1989	29	5	14	19	2
1990	29	9	18	23	1
1991	29	4	14	21	1
1992	29	1	6	15	12
1993	30	6	17	21	1
1994	31	4	20	25	1
1995	31	5	19	23	2
1996	31	2	13	17	4
1997	32	0	7	16	5
1998	33	1	5	13	8
1999	34	3	7	21	7
2000	34	2	13	24	2

TOP FINISHES AT DAYTONA INTERNATIONAL SPEEDWAY

Victories, 125-mile Qualifying Race for the Daytona 500	Top Five Finishes, Daytona 500	Top-Five Finishes, Pepsi/Firecracker 400
1983	1980, 4th Place	1979, 3rd Place
1986	1981, 5th Place	1980, 3rd Place
1990	1984, 2nd Place	1988, 4th Place
1991	1987, 5th Place	1990, 1st Place
1992	1989, 3rd Place	1993, 1st Place
1993	1990, 5th Place	1994, 3rd Place
1994	1991, 5th Place	1995, 3rd Place
1995	1993, 2nd Place	1996, 4th Place
1996	1995, 2nd Place	1997, 4th Place
1997	1996, 2nd Place	1999, 2nd Place
1998	1998, 1st Place, 40th running of the Daytona 500 1999, 2nd Place	

Bibliography

Fielden, Greg. *Forty Years of Stock Car Racing*, vol. 1–4. Surfside Beach, South Carolina: Galfield Press, 1988, 1989, 1990.

——. *Forty Years of Stock Car Racing: Forty Plus Four*. Surfside Beach, South Carolina: Galfield Press, 1994.

——, and Peter Golenbock. *Stock Car Racing Encyclopedia*. New York: Macmillan, 1997.

Moriarty, Frank. *Sunday Drivers: NASCAR Winston Cup Stock Car Racing*. Charlottesville, Virginia: Howell Press, 1994.

——. *The Encyclopedia of Stock Car Racing*. New York: MetroBooks, 1998.

Various. *Goodwrench Service Racing Media Guide*.

Various. *NASCAR Winston Cup Series Media Guide*. Winston-Salem, North Carolina: Sports Marketing Enterprises, various years.

Various writers of *The Charlotte Observer*. *Dale Earnhardt: Rear View Mirror*. Champaign, Illinois: Sports Publishing Incorporated, 1998.

Vehorn, Frank. *The Intimidator*, 4th ed. Asheboro, North Carolina: Down Home Press, 1999.